PRAISE FOR *BENEATH THE SURFACE*

"*Beneath the Surface* is critical to any parent, whether or not the parent realizes it. As a man who never took one psychology course, I appreciate that Kristi Hugstad wrote about a serious topic in a way that I could embrace and learn from. This book not only changed my life, it changed the life of my child."

— **Kevin Thaddeus Fisher-Paulson**,
columnist, *San Francisco Chronicle*

"Exploring everything from the addictive effects of excessive video gaming to the warning signs of alcohol and drug abuse, Kristi Hugstad leaves no stone unturned in her quest to raze the stigma of depression. She does so in a way that is effective, accessible, and highly informative. A must-read for anyone wanting permission to help themselves or a friend, this book reads as though it's reaching out to grab you and hold you in your time of need."

— **Regina Louise**, author of *Somebody's Someone*

"Each year as a high school teacher, I see more and more students struggling with depression, anxiety, and overwhelming stress. *Beneath the Surface* is a powerful work that uncovers the growing epidemic of pressures facing adolescents today and offers the tools necessary to help students navigate these pressures directly. Kristi Hugstad's writing eloquently and accessibly captures the depth of these issues through her own story as well as the stories of others. When you find yourself wondering what you can do, or you have a student who is struggling, here is a book that can help. It is a starting point for a conversation that just might save someone's life."

— **William Mever**, author of *Three Breaths and Begin*

"In *Beneath the Surface*, Kristi Hugstad writes about how to recognize the warning signs of depression and suicide and shares valuable resources that we can all use to prevent suicide. As a college professor who interacts with young students on a daily basis, I experience how the epidemic of stress and poor mental health is affecting the personal and professional lives of my students. This is a must-read for high school and college students, parents, healthcare providers, and educators. Read this book — and apply it."
— **Mahtab Jafari**, professor of pharmaceutical sciences,
University of California, Irvine

"*Beneath the Surface* is a well-written outreach mainly to adolescents, but frankly to anyone seeking to help a family member or friend suffering with depression and suicidal ideation. Kristi Hugstad struggles to come to grips with her own riveting experience of losing a husband who completed suicide despite her best efforts. Hugstad weaves together science, psychology, and social connections by relating the poignant stories of adolescents suffering from depression. The book describes groupings of common clinical manifestations of depression to provide a guidepost to assist teenagers and others who come into contact with adolescents with malignant suicidal ideation. She provides scientific knowledge and her own experience to promote awareness and offer tools for dealing with deep depression and high suicide risk. A great read that's clinically relevant and helpful."
— **Nadine Levinson**, DDS, clinical professor, psychiatry,
University of California, Irvine, School of Medicine; training
and supervising psychoanalyst, San Diego Psychoanalytic Center

"As I know from personal experience, the teenage years are often the most difficult and challenging in a human being's life. This book offers invaluable insight and support that will help any troubled teen come through the turbulence of those years."
— **Steve Taylor**, PhD, author of *The Leap* and *The Calm Center*

Beneath the Surface

Beneath
the Surface

A Teen's Guide to Reaching Out
When You or Your Friend Is in Crisis

KRISTI HUGSTAD

Foreword by Nancy Guerra, EdD

New World Library
Novato, California

New World Library
14 Pamaron Way
Novato, California 94949

The material in this book is intended for education. It is not meant to take the place of diagnosis and treatment by a qualified medical practitioner or therapist. No expressed or implied guarantee of the effects of the use of the recommendations can be given or liability taken.

Text design by Tona Pearce Myers

Library of Congress Cataloging-in-Publication data is available.

First printing, September 2019
ISBN 978-1-60868-635-3
Ebook ISBN 978-1-60868-636-0
Printed in Canada on 100% postconsumer-waste recycled paper

New World Library is proud to be a Gold Certified Environmentally Responsible Publisher. Publisher certification awarded by Green Press Initiative.

10   9   8   7   6   5   4   3   2   1

*For struggling teens everywhere —
you are not alone*

The most beautiful people we have known are those who have known defeat, known suffering, known struggle, known loss, and have found their way out of the depths. These persons have an appreciation, a sensitivity, and an understanding of life that fills them with compassion, gentleness, and a deep loving concern.

— Elisabeth Kübler-Ross

CONTENTS

FOREWORD

As a mother and a psychologist who studies adolescent development, I know how difficult the teen years can be. Not only do teens often face the stressors of daily life, from financial concerns to relationship problems to family struggles, they also face a separate set of challenges related to their age and stage in life — adolescence is a unique time when we transition between childhood and adulthood. This means that, in addition to normal stressors, teens have challenges *just because* they are teenagers. I certainly saw this in my own children. Indeed, by middle school, and certainly by high school, my children struggled with self-doubt, wondering whether their friends approved of their every move, wanting to belong to the popular group, and trying to figure out who they were and what they wanted to do next. They struggled with decisions and how to manage their emotions, often reacting impulsively without realizing that one bad decision could have devastating consequences.

My children and their friends certainly were not unique. These challenges are shared by most teens around the world. They can also lead to serious mental health problems, including anxiety, depression, substance abuse, and self-harm. What's more, many of these challenges continue beyond the teen years into early adulthood. I see undergraduates in my classes experiencing stress levels off the charts, plagued by self-doubt, uncertainty about the future, and high levels of depression and anxiety, even to the point of wondering if they can go on. Yet so many teenagers and young adults face these challenges without asking for help from anyone, as if asking for help were a sign of weakness. Or possibly they think no one else could know or understand what they are going through. But believe me, everyone has a story; so many of us have battled with our own fears and demons, and there are solutions. Teens who have gone through these struggles and have found their way back through determination and resilience have inspirational stories. Adults who have lived through heartbreaking and devastating events talk about how these experiences have left them wiser and stronger. Researchers who study mental health and well-being have insights into what works best for prevention and treatment.

So many of us are searching for solutions — for help and hope for ourselves, our friends, and our children and families. *Beneath the Surface* can help you find these solutions. Kristi has written a truly amazing book that brings together her own tragic experience of her husband's suicide, compelling stories from teenagers highlighting resilience and strength in the face of despair, and the most current research to help you understand adolescent development and mental illness risk, prevention, and treatment. Kristi is living proof that we can live happy lives in spite of difficult and even life-shattering events. She shares this with you and outlines a clear path to learn and practice hope.

Beneath the Surface draws from Kristi's compassion for others, but it also provides many useful tips, activities, practices, and suggestions for getting out from behind the darkness, for creating a life story of positive change and personal growth, and for engaging others in your journey. She provides a wealth of solid advice that is supported by research, but this book is more than an academic review of current studies or a self-help manual. Kristi writes from the heart. She brilliantly weaves together current research, her own personal experiences, and firsthand stories from youth. When you read this book, you feel like you are communicating directly with Kristi, that she cares about *you,* and I believe she truly does. She cares deeply about all young people and about humankind. This book doesn't just teach you how to change, it inspires you to change.

Dr. Nancy Guerra
Professor of Psychological Science
Dean, School of Social Ecology
University of California, Irvine

INTRODUCTION

GAVIN'S STORY

Hi, my name is Gavin, and in short, I'm lucky to be alive today.

I suffer from depression, and I've been seriously suicidal, yet I'm still here, right now, today, and I'm actually happy. But that wasn't always the case.

Why am I still here? Or more importantly, how?

I'm here because I got treatment for my depression. Once I realized I had this illness and got help for it, life got better.

But I've gotten ahead of myself.

When I was just four years old, my dad died from lung cancer. I remember visiting him in the hospital, having no clue what was going on (how could I? I was only four), and then one day, my dad was just gone. Forever. I can't recall a single childhood birthday party. My mom struggled as a single mother to raise my two brothers and me. I know it wasn't easy for her or for any of us.

By the time I got to middle school, I had severe depression and anxiety, but I didn't know it. I had no desire to go to school, and when I got home, all I did was sleep. I went to counseling, but it didn't help my depression. The older I got, the darker my world got. In high school, I began to use benzos — or benzodiazepines — and other prescription drugs. They gave me some immediate relief, but that didn't last.

If I had to sum it up, I'd say I felt like I was a total waste of space. I felt as if I didn't have a purpose. I was suicidal. I went to the top of a parking structure in Mission Viejo, California. Jumping off seemed like the best way to escape my pain. It wasn't that I wanted to end my life so much as I wanted to stop hurting so badly on the inside.

I'll never forget that moment, standing at the top of that structure, four stories from an end to my pain. If you had told me then that I could one day feel happy and healthy, I wouldn't have believed it.

I have felt as bad as you might be feeling now — and probably worse — but I was able to turn my life around using the same information and advice you'll read in this book, which can help you recognize and work through depression, anxiety, and so many other issues and conditions we teens face all the time. Picking it up is a first huge step.

Keep reading.

BENEATH THE SURFACE OF TEEN LIFE

Being a teenager in this day and age is totally exhausting.

Your parents and teachers were once teenagers (hard to believe, right?), but they didn't have laptops, smartphones, and social media. They didn't have to *keep up*. So they get it, but maybe not entirely, not the way you do because you're *in* it. And you're in deep — you can't avoid it — you can't just *not* be who you are or where you are! There are times you just want to go in your bedroom, shut the door, and not have to deal with anyone ever again.

It's only human to reach your breaking point some-times with people, school, friends, family, *life*. But when that breaking point feels like a tunnel without a light at the end, when it feels like you are very alone and no one cares, when it feels like you are only spiraling further downward, that's cause for concern — that's when a problem might be hard to solve completely on your own. That's when you need help — which is totally okay. Everyone — poor, rich, old, young, from every background and ethnicity — needs help in life once in a while. No one can go it alone all the way.

I have written this book specifically for teenagers in crisis, and that's who I often address throughout. But in fact, this book is for anyone — teen or parent, teacher or coach — who knows a teen who may be struggling with de-pression or suicide. Whether you are reading this book for yourself or to help a friend or family member, I hope I can help you find the information you need.

Why do I think I can help? Bill, my husband, completed suicide.

Yes, you read that right.

It was awful, horrible, painful. In fact, words will never be able to accurately describe the experience, which I share near the end of the book. That experience has made me want to help people who suffer from depression and may be considering suicide — or who know someone who suffers from depression and is suicidal — to find the appropriate treatment in order to feel better.

Depression is a disease of the mind. When you understand that, it loses some of its power. Yes, depression is very real and very scary, and suicidal thoughts can make someone feel frightened and overwhelmed. A depressed person might think they're "going crazy" or feel embarrassed to share with others what they are thinking. Or they might try to talk about how they feel but others don't take them seriously. Or maybe the people they talk to don't know what to say, so they just say nothing.

If this is happening to you, don't give up. Talking about depressive or suicidal thoughts and feelings with the *right* person makes all the difference in the world.

When you're in a scary place, you're always better off when you are with someone.

Unfortunately, nearly forty-five thousand Americans die by suicide each year. That's a lot of suffering. The truth is, many of us think about suicide at one time or another in our lives. This can happen when we are struggling with overwhelming problems that make us feel trapped and hopeless. We don't genuinely want to die. We want to stop feeling so miserable, and bad feelings can sometimes *feel* permanent. But they *aren't*. All feelings can change, though sometimes we need help to change them. Suicide is what can't be taken back; the consequences are permanent.

Further, people don't need to have "bad things" happen to them to become depressed. Did you know that the modern conveniences of smartphones and social media can actually contribute to feelings of anxiety and insecurity? It's true. Social media has been linked both to depression and to behaviors that are either risk factors or symptoms of depression: insomnia, bullying, inability to concentrate, and low self-esteem.

How does this happen? On social media, it's impossible to have anonymity or control over what others say. It's also easy to (inadvertently) compare ourselves to others, especially when peers post about their lives — even when we know that people carefully curate what they show and that a few characters, sentences, or pictures never tell the whole story. We may feel our life doesn't measure up, and yet we want our peers' approval and are afraid of losing it. Depending on someone else's approval can make anyone feel vulnerable and increase anxiety. This is normal but not helpful, particularly for someone who's already struggling with depression.

Thus, social media connects us in many wonderful ways, but it also can feed the very fears that lead to depression and a sense of hopelessness. If this speaks to your experience, and you feel scared to admit your feelings to your parents, teachers, or peers, know that it's okay. There's nothing wrong with you. Don't give yourself a hard time for being scared. What you need, like Gavin, is help, and I hope this book can start you on your way.

Each chapter addresses a different cause or aspect of depression and suicidal thoughts. Many of these causes or issues are a normal part of growing up. Dealing with them can be hard, but the good news is that they can all be handled. However, sometimes their scale, frequency, and combination can lead to more dangerous problems. Serious depression is an illness that requires treatment, but it *can* be treated.

Using real-life examples of young people who have suffered depression firsthand, I'll help you recognize the risk factors and warning signs. I will also dispel some of the myths about teen suicide. Teens today experience some complex issues, all of which may be caused by or may contribute to depression or other mental illnesses. This book offers information on eating disorders, anxiety, substance abuse, self-harm, bullying, technology addiction, peer and academic pressures, and post-traumatic stress disorder (PTSD). I also include practical exercises that will help you identify quickly and confidently whether you or someone you know is in need of help and, if so, what to do.

Finally, I share the story of my husband's suicide. At the time of Bill's death, I didn't recognize the risk factors or understand the warning signs. Perhaps if I had, his story may have turned out differently. Knowing how critical it is to understand these topics, I've provided discussion questions at the end of the book to help you reflect on and apply this information.

My hope is that this book helps you or someone you love write a good story. That story won't be full of only positive experiences. The road of life is tough — that's an inevitable part of life! — but by meeting the challenges we face, we can learn and grow from them, which only makes us stronger. First and foremost, don't beat yourself up for struggling or having certain feelings. Depression is no one's fault. There is help, and there is hope!

Chapter 1

<hr>

WHAT'S GOING ON IN YOUR BRAIN?

It's an age-old problem: Parents don't understand their teen, teens don't understand their parents, and both groups wonder why the other can't just see things their way. Sound familiar?

If you feel like your brain works differently than your parents', teachers', or any other adult's, there's a good reason — it does! The teen brain isn't just an adult brain with less experience. It's a brain that *functions* differently than an adult brain.

The first thing you should know is that a teenager's brain hasn't finished developing yet. In fact, it won't be considered "mature" until sometime between age twenty-five and thirty. Think about that; teens make some of life's most important decisions — like where to go to college, what career to pursue, perhaps even who to marry — before their brain is fully developed. So while adults might dismiss "irrational" teen choices and behavior by blaming it on raging hormones or peer pressure, teens are simply reacting and responding based on their brain's current functionality (not to say teens aren't affected by hormones!).

As the brain develops, it does so from the back forward. The *reptilian* portion, or the back of the brain, is the first to mature. This is the area of the brain responsible for the most basic human instincts. In a nutshell, it's what keeps you (and the human species) alive. This is where fight-or-flight instincts arise as well as the innate urge to reproduce. This area isn't logical or emotional; it's all about self-preservation.

The middle of the brain, also called the limbic or second brain, develops next. This area is responsible for memory, emotion, pleasure, connection, love, and trust. The second brain determines your mood and helps you balance your self-interest with your concern for others. Think about it like this: A toddler might hit a friend to get a toy back, but as we grow, we begin to notice the needs of others and will at times (though certainly not always!) sacrifice some of our innate self-interest on their behalf.

The front region of the brain, called the cortical brain, matures last. This is the area responsible for logic, reasoning, rational thinking, organization, and decision-making. The cortical brain is divided into lobes with various functions and responsibilities. This section is the "newest" portion of the brain, evolutionarily speaking. Basically, the reptilian and limbic brains are structurally very similar to those of the first humans. But the cortical brain is different. It enables higher thinking. The only catch is that it takes a few decades to mature.

That brings us to where you are right now. Teens have a

fully functioning reptilian brain, and the limbic brain matures rapidly around puberty, when it experiences a lot of change. I don't have to tell you that; after all, you're alive and you're feeling *all* the feels. What's different about the teen brain is that the front part is still in a state of plasticity — meaning it's changing all the time. This can be a huge advantage in some ways. The brain's plasticity allows teens to change and adapt based on circumstances. This state is perfect for absorbing information; that's why children and adolescents learn languages and music more easily than adults.

Of course, there's a catch. Basically, the different areas of the brain mature at different rates. The connections between your frontal cortex, where rational thinking and decision-making occur, and your limbic system, where emotions arise, strengthen through age and experience. But during the teen years, those areas don't communicate optimally, and consequently, teens might make decisions or behave in ways that their parents or other adults simply don't understand. Scientists believe this is why teens are so much more prone to risk-taking and recklessness than mature adults. Additionally, teens feel mature, grown-up feelings in one part of the brain that another part of the brain cannot yet fully process. That puts teens in a tough, and often confusing, state of mind (literally).

So when teens multitask to get everything done — do chores, ask parents to sign forms, be at practice on Saturday morning, write an essay Thursday night, study for a Friday quiz, clean their room — well...it can be completely daunting. Really, it's no wonder if you forget about a quiz and your bedroom floor is covered in clothing. The life of a teen is overwhelming no matter how good their organizational skills and how developed their brain!

However, in addition to understanding the teen brain, it's also important to understand the parental brain. All brains are hardwired for survival — to doing whatever is necessary to keep ourselves alive. But a parent's brain is also wired to keep *their child (you!),* alive. Scientific research shows that both men and women experience changes in their brain and endocrine systems (where hormones are created) after having a child — whether biologically or through adoption. The instincts formed through these changes provide parents with one *major* goal: to do whatever is necessary to protect their child. Moms and dads — and really all loving adult caretakers — are *wired* to do what's best for their children, though it may seem they are only trying to make decisions for you or to nag and control you. Whether or not they *actually* know and do what's best, protecting their children is usually their motivation.

Your teen years really are a time of discovery. You're learning and growing and discovering who you are. That's because your brain is doing the same thing. Your brain is still developing, and its three parts are still figuring out how to work together in a balanced, effective way — so that no part has too much or too little power. However, it hasn't figured this out yet, which is why outside stressors and behaviors can alter that balance and cause problems. For example, everyone desires reward and seeks pleasure, emotions that live in the limbic brain. But the brain's reward center is kind of on overdrive during the teen years. This area is driven by dopamine, a chemical that makes us feel good. This feeling is important to everyone, but it's vital to teens. That's why impulsivity and giving in to peer pressure are so common for teens. The desire for pleasure and approval often surpasses other instincts and abilities, including the fear response in the reptilian brain that's wired to protect you and keep you alive. When this happens too often, reward-driven behavior can become addictive, even when you know what you're doing is dangerous and harmful, such as taking drugs. This is why addiction often starts in the teen years. When left unchecked, the limbic brain can eventually take over, overshadowing even someone's survival instincts, rational thinking, and decision-making abilities, which is why addicts behave in such reckless, life-threatening ways.

Of course, as an adult with a fully developed brain, you will eventually have a better perspective as well as better decision-making ability — but that doesn't make the here and now much easier, does it? If you struggle making decisions, or always seem to make the wrong ones, know that's part of the process. And don't underestimate your parents and other caring adults in your life. They've been where you are, and they remember it all too well. No matter how it may seem, they want to protect you and help you be as happy and healthy as possible.

And that's exactly what I hope this book does — helps you be as happy and healthy as you can be.

Chapter 2

YOU ARE NOT ALONE

Most children grow up thinking their home, family, and upbringing are "normal," even when they're not. Children and teens living in a home where one or both parents are depressed often don't realize this isn't the norm — though this situation is more common than you may think.

In fact, fifteen *million* kids in the United States have parents with depression.

As a result, these fifteen million kids are at greater risk of developing depression themselves. But depression can happen to anyone. It can occur after a trauma or during a stressful situation, or it can develop due to someone's particular brain chemistry. *Why* someone develops depression is important, particularly if it's due to situational or lifestyle factors, which can be changed. But more important than the *why* is the *how*. As in, how do you deal with depression? That is the real focus of this book because depression can put someone at risk for any number of issues, including suicide.

The faster you recognize the symptoms of depression, the faster you can get treatment and reduce the risk of other, even more serious issues. Additionally, the more you know, the better you can help others.

Are you at risk for depression? Consider the following questions, all of which may indicate that someone is already depressed or at risk for developing depression. If you find yourself answering affirmatively even to several questions, it doesn't necessarily mean you're depressed, but you may have an increased risk of becoming so. Later we'll talk about what you can do if you or someone you love is suffering from depression.

DEPRESSION SELF-ASSESSMENT

Do you currently live with a family member who suffers from depression?

Studies have shown that living with a mother or father who has depression, whether the cause is environmental or genetic, increases your own risk of developing the condition. You may not know if a parent suffers from depression; if you feel safe asking, do so. If not, consider whether they exhibit the signs described in this book. Further, you don't have to live with a depressed family member to be at risk.

Does life feel pointless?

Everyone may occasionally feel hopeless as they navigate through school, work, and life. But if a hopeless feeling persists day after day and affects your daily behavior, it could be a sign of depression.

Do you find it impossible to concentrate?

Depression can make it hard to concentrate even when you're reading or watching something you love.

Have you withdrawn from your friends and family?

It's important to do your own thing and be independent, but this should be balanced with a healthy amount of socializing and bonding with friends and family. Depression sufferers often turn down opportunities to be with others simply to be alone.

Have you noticed a sudden change in your weight?

Extreme weight loss or gain can be a symptom of depression. If you've lost your appetite or find yourself seeking comfort in food, this may be because your brain chemistry is being affected by depression.

Do you have insomnia, or do you sleep too much?

Look, teenagers need their sleep and often don't get enough. But if you go through long periods of sleeplessness or of sleeping too much, depression may be the reason.

Do you have physical pain that won't go away?

Depression doesn't just cause emotional pain. Depression can cause chemical imbalances in your brain that make you perceive pain differently, and it could be the reason for a persistent physical pain that doctors can't find a reason for.

Have your grades dropped? Have you stopped participating in extracurriculars?

Depression has two best friends: apathy and lack of energy. These can combine to affect your performance in school and your extracurricular activities, and they can sap your passion for activities you once loved.

Have you ever thought of suicide?

If you answer yes, you're not alone, and suicidal thoughts can be caused by depression. However, if you're *currently* thinking about suicide, seek help and treatment. Tell someone. With counseling and, if necessary, proper medication, you will begin to feel better. When you're suffering from depression, the idea of feeling better might be difficult to imagine. This is the time to practice trust and courage. For immediate help, see the organizations listed in the resources section at the back of this book (page 145).

Chapter 3

DEPRESSION

Depression refers to feelings of intense sadness that don't go away after a few hours or even a few days. It's not feeling sad when things go wrong, which is expected; it's feeling sad all the time, when everything is going *right*, too.

Depression affects a person's thoughts in such a way that they don't see when or how a problem can be overcome. It leads people to focus mostly on failures and disappointments and to emphasize only the negative side of their situation. Someone with severe depression is unable to see the possibility of a good outcome and may believe he or she will never be happy or that things will never be right for them again.

Looking on the "bright side" is often impossible for someone suffering from depression. Depression is like wearing sunglasses in an already dark room: It completely distorts your thinking. That's why depressed people often can't recognize that their perspective is limited or obscured and that emotional problems are temporary and changeable, so they turn to the permanent solution of suicide. Someone with depression may feel like there's no other way out, no other escape from emotional pain, and no other way to communicate desperate unhappiness. They lose hope that their mood will ever improve. They lose the ability, after feeling down for a long time, to step back and view their situation objectively.

Sometimes people who feel suicidal may not even realize they are depressed. When depression causes someone to see all situations in a negative way, suicidal thinking is a real concern.

It's important to remember that there isn't a standard form of depression. No two brains are exactly alike, and since depression is a disease of the brain, there will never be two identical cases. Additionally, the distinct details of someone's life and situation affect the ways in which the disease manifests itself, though the feelings of hopelessness are often similar. Here is Jackie's story, which is about when she was a teenager in Baton Rouge, Louisiana.

JACKIE'S STORY

I always knew I was different than other girls. Not only was I taller and stronger, I also felt comfortable playing sports with boys, I refused to wear skirts or dresses, and I preferred to keep my hair short. In school during recess or other athletic events, I'd sometimes hang back, out of fear I'd be teased for "acting like a boy." That had happened to me before, and it was really hurtful.

My father is an alcoholic, and my mom is my best friend, but she's nothing like me — she used to be a dancer, and she's won beauty pageants. She loves to obsess over fad diets, exercise videos, and food portions. Whenever I didn't feel good about myself or my body, I was too ashamed to share my feelings with my mom because I thought she would judge me.

At the time, I was actually suffering from what I later learned is called gender confusion. This gave me anxiety, which then morphed into depression. Again, I didn't know there were names for the things I was feeling at the time; I just knew I felt really crappy, and I felt like something was wrong with me. I felt like my body and my gender didn't match. I couldn't deal with the stress, and I felt like my parents really cared about my appearance. So, in an effort to be the "perfect female," I vomited after I ate, alternating through unhealthy periods of bingeing followed by violent purging. This is called bulimia.

Well, bulimia didn't help my self-esteem. Every time I looked in the mirror, all I felt was guilty — guilty about who I am, what I was eating, how I looked, and how the rest of the world perceived me. I thought that if I told my parents how I really felt about myself and my body, they would be disappointed in me or even angry with me.

Instead of asking for help, I turned to food and substances as coping mechanisms. At times of extreme depression, I binged on foods I knew were off-limits: donuts, French fries, and milkshakes. Then, I'd vomit as much as I could and vow to start over again. To help curb my appetite, I began using a prescription stimulant that I was able to buy from kids at school.

Throughout high school, I continued to slip into a deep clinical depression. Every day, I felt like I would never live up to what everyone else expected of me and that I could never share my bad feelings because everything I felt was wrong.

When I graduated high school, I moved away from my hometown to attend college, and in the anonymity of my new surroundings, I finally felt I could become who I really am. I went to student health services, and they referred me to a psychologist, who diagnosed me with gender dysphoria, in addition to the bulimia I knew I had, which explained why I didn't feel like *me* — I felt more male than female. I then sought out support groups for gender dysphoria and eating disorders, where I met other students to whom I could relate. Slowly, I began the process of accepting myself for who I really am. I began eating healthier and better. Slowly, I was able to look in the mirror and accept my size and shape as *mine*.

You might be surprised to learn that today I'm the chief financial officer of a thriving business in Minneapolis, Minnesota. My own struggles growing up propelled me to become an activist in the LGBTQ community. And because I don't want anyone to have to go through what I did, I volunteer with organizations dedicated to helping teens and young adults with eating disorders.

My advice to you is simple:

- Never be ashamed of who you are.
- Accept yourself as you are, right now.
- Don't tolerate judgment from others, just as you would not judge in return.
- Practice self-care.
- Strive to be the best person you can be by being more compassionate and helpful to others.
- Get outside yourself. The smallest act of kindness will do wonders for your self-pride.

SYMPTOMS OF DEPRESSION

Jackie's story lists several symptoms of depression. Do you or does someone you know demonstrate any of them?

- Loss of interest in previously fun activities
- Conflict or fights with family or friends
- Low self-esteem
- Complaints of pain, including headaches, stomachaches, low back pain, or fatigue
- Difficulty concentrating, making decisions, or remembering things
- Excessive or inappropriate guilt
- Irresponsible behavior: skipping school, class tardiness, forgetfulness
- Loss of interest in food or compulsive overeating
- Preoccupation with death, dying, and suicide
- Rebellious behavior
- Sadness, anxiety, or feelings of hopelessness
- Staying awake at night and sleeping during the day
- Sudden drop in grades
- Use of alcohol or drugs
- Promiscuous sexual activity
- Withdrawal from friends and family
- Crying for no apparent reason
- Feelings of anger, even over small things
- Fixation on past failures, self-criticism, or self-blame
- Feeling that life and the future are grim and bleak

ASK THE QUESTION

What might Jackie's high school experience have been like if someone, at some point, had asked her the right question? If you think someone is depressed, you can begin a conversation with that person by simply asking, "Are you okay?" Because getting *beneath the surface*, first and foremost, requires asking.

Believe it or not, teens who are depressed or considering suicide are usually willing to talk if someone asks them, out of genuine concern and care, if they are okay. When you take a brave step to start a conversation with these three words, you open the door to encourage someone to get the help they need.

When someone is depressed, they are not able to see the answers or solutions to problems clearly. That's when speaking with a trusted friend or relative can help the person recognize or identify healthy ways out of a bad situation. Sometimes finding that light in the tunnel starts with a simple conversation.

If a friend or family member opens up to you, know that takes courage and trust. But that trust does not — and should not — swear you to silence. If the topic of suicide arises, whatever you do, whatever you think, whatever you say, this is one time to not keep secrets.

In fact, if a friend or classmate swears you to secrecy, get them help immediately; tell an adult you trust as soon as possible! For more advice on helping someone else, see chapter 15.

People who have depression are also at risk for a number of other issues. As you know, depression is caused by both genetics and environmental factors, but depression can be caused by, and be the *cause of,* several other issues and conditions, which the next several chapters focus on. This list is not exhaustive, but it includes the more common issues teenagers face today — issues that can have a significant impact on your mental health and happiness.

Chapter 4

EATING DISORDERS

It's just food, right? While that statement seems simple, for many people — particularly teens — a healthy relationship with food is a lofty wish. Like Jackie in chapter 3, many teens today suffer from eating disorders, also called disordered eating. Eating disorders can range from anorexia (avoidance of food) to bulimia (inducing vomiting after eating) to binge eating and compulsive overeating. Although eating disorders are more common in young females, males are also at risk, particularly those who are athletes. Even teens who do not suffer from an eating disorder might occasionally have a preoccupation with food, weight loss, restrictive eating behavior, or food phobias. While eating disorders can affect anyone, some people are more at risk. These include people who are or have the following:

- Close relatives with (or a family history of) eating disorders

- Family members who exhibit a preoccupation with diet and weight loss
- Family history of mental illness
- A perfectionist personality
- A history of anxiety
- Experience with weight-based bullying or discrimination
- LGBTQ youth
- Small or unsupportive social network

Eating disorders are diseases, but they're also coping mechanisms. Like alcoholism or drug abuse, an eating disorder might be used to cope with one or more underlying issues or conditions. Controlling food intake or physical appearance could be someone's way of taking control when life seems out of control. It might be a way to relieve stress or to distract from other painful issues. If you're dealing with an eating disorder, you might panic at the thought of treating it, since it might be the one thing in your life that makes you feel safe and secure. In fact, an eating disorder may be such a big part of someone's life that it seems impossible to go on without it.

However, obviously, all humans require proper nutrition to function properly — for a healthy body and mind — but diet can also play a huge role in treating mental illness (which I discuss later). In fact, *eating disorders have the highest mortality rate of any mental illness.* Think about that; statistically, having an eating disorder makes you more likely to *die.* That's not just because of the health implications of starving or depriving oneself of proper nutrition (although this causes the majority of eating disorder–related deaths).

Among those suffering from anorexia, one in every five deaths is from suicide.

Since everyone has different eating habits, it can be difficult to determine whether you or someone you love is suffering from an eating disorder. The following common signs and symptoms can help you recognize the illness:

- Distorted body image (seeing yourself differently than others see you)
- Frequent or constant feelings of hunger
- Avoidance of events or situations that include food
- Social isolation or withdrawal
- Thinning hair, dry skin, and broken nails
- Unexplained skipped menstrual periods
- Preoccupation with calorie counting
- Irritability, anxiety, or depression
- Eating in secret

EATING DISORDER STATISTICS

If you think you suffer from an eating disorder, you're not alone. In fact, it's estimated that thirty million people of all ages and genders suffer from an eating disorder. Additionally, the National Association of Anorexia Nervosa publishes these statistics:

- At least one person dies almost hourly as a direct result of an eating disorder.
- Sixteen percent of transgender college students report having an eating disorder.

- Nearly 1 percent of all American women will suffer from anorexia sometime in their life.
- Fifty to 80 percent of the risk for anorexia and bulimia is genetic.
- Thirty-three to 50 percent of anorexia patients have a mood disorder, like depression, and about half have an anxiety disorder.

GETTING HELP

The statistics show the link between eating disorders and conditions like depression and anxiety. This is important because eating disorders usually aren't solitary conditions. Most teens, like Jackie, who suffer from an eating disorder are also suffering from other psychiatric disorders or mental health issues.

Untreated, an eating disorder *and* the underlying issues causing it can wreak havoc on someone's health, happiness, and self-esteem — basically on every facet of your life. If you suspect you or someone you love has an eating disorder, don't hesitate. Get help immediately. The guidelines later in this book for living your healthiest life are no substitute for professional help when you need it. Professional counseling or therapy is the best way to work through and heal from an eating disorder. If you don't know who to talk to, try the adult you feel closest to (and see the resources in the back of this book). Is there a parent, an aunt or uncle, a teacher, a coach, or a religious leader you can speak to? Take the risk to open up; your well-being is worth it. An eating disorder, like depression, often leads to feelings of hopelessness.

But remember: *There is always hope.*

Chapter 5

BULLYING

Sticks and stones can break your bones...and words can absolutely destroy. Bullying is not only a schoolyard problem. It can be a potentially life-threatening issue at any age. That's because bullying — whether it's done by peers, friends, relatives, coworkers, or adults — aims to degrade someone's character and destroy their self-esteem. Low self-esteem and self-confidence are risk factors for depression and many other mental illnesses. There's a reason that teens who are bullied are more likely to consider suicide than those who are not. Words are powerful and can undermine someone's will to live, which kills just as effectively as physical injury.

CAITLIN'S STORY

When my sister, Sofia, completed suicide, no one saw it coming. Being five years older, I was in college the year she decided to take her life. My parents, her school counselors, her friends, and her teachers were unaware of the pain my sister was suffering from on a daily basis. Unfortunately, when she decided she couldn't take it anymore, no one was there to stop her.

Two years before Sofia's suicide, my family moved from a small town in Northern California to a large suburb of Los Angeles. Sofia was fifteen, a freshman in high school, and had always had a good group of friends. She was pretty and popular in our hometown. When she started school after our move, she struggled to fit in. She was still friendly and pretty, but her grade was filled with cliques of girls who were unwilling to befriend new girls. Even worse, they wanted to make sure Sofia knew she didn't belong.

Since she was four or five, Sofia wore glasses to help her see far away. Suddenly, her glasses were a target for abuse. The girls near her locker called her a nerd and said she was even uglier without the glasses than she was with them. In gym class, another group of girls made fun of Sofia because of her small breasts and boyish figure. They teased her constantly, telling her she should change in the boy's locker room.

Online, the bullying was even worse. Sofia's classmates used anonymous or hidden social media accounts to terrorize her. Classmates would take photos of her in the locker room and post them online. Sometimes, she'd receive threatening messages telling her if she didn't kill herself, someone else would do her a favor and do it for her.

My little sister was absolutely miserable. Unfortunately, we didn't know it. While she gradually became more and more withdrawn, she didn't tell me or our parents about the bullying. She spent more time in her room, sleeping when-ever possible. Sofia had always been a smart, successful student. Suddenly, she was pulling Cs and incompletes in her favorite classes. After her death, we discovered So-fia's ankles bore dozens of scars that appeared to be self-inflicted cuts.

When Sofia no longer wanted to go to school, our par-ents thought she was going through a phase of teenage angst. They told her she needed to try to make friends and work harder on her grades. Inside, Sofia was dying, but we weren't able to give her the help she so desper-ately needed. If Sofia had had a close friend in her school, perhaps he or she would have told us what was going on — or told anyone. But instead, Sofia was completely alone.

One day she decided she couldn't take it anymore. She wrote a letter to me and one to our parents before she hanged herself in her bedroom. The letters simply said that she loved us and was sorry. It wasn't until later we dis-covered what was happening to her at school and online.

Sofia's death didn't need to happen. There are so many people who could have or would have helped her. But Sofia felt so isolated and alone that she wasn't able to go to any of us. And we failed to see the warning signs that now seem so obvious.

If there's one thing I hope can come of her death, it's that anyone reading this takes the risk factors and warn-ing signs of suicide seriously. And that they never, ever engage in bullying another person. Those words, threats, and insults have more power than you think. They do more than hurt; they can kill.

WHAT IS BULLYING?

Bullying is unsolicited harassment and aggression. It involves violence — either physical or psychological — aimed at a person or group of people. While anyone may occasionally argue or fight with a friend or peer, bullying is underscored by a more insidious intent. In a nutshell, a bully is actively and strategically trying to inflict pain and suffering on another person, most often someone they already know or have a relationship with (though usually not a close relationship).

Bullying takes many forms. It can include insults, name-calling, shaming, belittling, pushing, hitting, threatening, and public embarrassment. Bullying behavior is usually repeated, and this repetition can quickly become psychologically damaging. Bullies often feel they have superiority over their victim for some reason, whether that's due to physical appearance, popularity, age, intelligence, race, sex, ethnicity, or socioeconomic status. This sense of superiority may exist only in the bully's mind and have no basis in reality, but bullies use it to gain power over their victims.

Cyberbullying

Today, much of our social lives occurs online, so bullying also occurs there. Cyberbullying is bullying that happens via social media, text messages, and other forms of digital communication. In Sofia's case, she received anonymous threats online, and bullies used social media to publicly humiliate her by posting embarrassing and inappropriate photos.

A one-time insult or rude remark on social media is not cyberbullying. As with all bullying, cyberbullying refers to repeated acts that intend to cause harm. Cyberbullying can be particularly harmful because it's easier to hide. Bullies are often strategic in covering their tracks, allowing them to bully their victims secretly and avoid being caught.

THE IMPACT OF BULLYING

Bullying — despite what some may say — is not just part of growing up. Rather, bullying can have devastating effects on its victims. Bullying can lead to insecurity, low self-esteem, depression, anxiety, and thoughts of suicide. According to the *Journal of the American Medical Association,* peer victimization and bullying cause higher rates of suicide, with cyberbullying specifically leading to more thoughts of suicide than traditional bullying.

Bullying has also changed. Talk to your parents or watch a teen movie from the eighties or nineties: Back then, the "bully" was usually a big guy pushing little guys around in the schoolyard or upending lunch trays in the cafeteria. Bullying happened face to face. Today, as you know, bullying can happen around the clock, from any location, thanks to the internet and social media, which increase the opportunity both to bully and to *be* bullied. According to Pew Research, 95 percent of teens own or have access to a smartphone, and 45 percent say they're online "almost constantly." With that in mind, the following statistics may not seem as shocking as they probably should:

- Twenty-eight percent of students in grades six to twelve experience bullying.

- Twenty percent of teens in grades nine to twelve experience bullying.
- Only one in five cyberbullying incidents are reported.
- Thirty percent of young people admit to bullying others.
- Around 70 percent of students and 70 percent of school staff report witnessing bullying.
- In 2017, 15 percent of teens in grades nine to twelve had been cyberbullied over the previous year.
- Fifty-five percent of LGBTQ students have experienced bullying.

BULLYING RISK FACTORS AND WARNING SIGNS

While bullying can happen to anyone, it is more common for teens and children who

- are overweight or underweight,
- are new students,
- are poor or in a lower socioeconomic class,
- suffer from depression or anxiety,
- are unpopular,
- are or are suspected to be LGBTQ,
- have low self-esteem,
- have few friends, or
- do not get along well with others.

As Caitlin described in her story, sometimes parents, siblings, and loved ones fail to notice the warning signs that someone is being bullied. Sofia, Caitlin's sister, exhibited many of the common warning signs for bullying. She withdrew from her friends and family and spent more time alone. Her grades dropped, even though she had been a good student before. She even bore the scars of self-injury. Teens who are being bullied sometimes try to conceal what's happening, and parents and adults can mistake behavioral changes for teenage moodiness. The following common warning signs are in fact quiet calls for help:

- Unexplained bruises or injuries
- Difficulty sleeping
- Frequent illness (stomachaches, headaches, feeling unwell)
- Skipping meals (especially lunches at school)
- Declining grades or academic performance
- The desire to stay home from school (or withdraw altogether)
- Lost or destroyed possessions, like clothes, shoes, electronics, and so on
- Loneliness or a lack of friends
- Self-injury, like cutting, burning, and hitting

Identifying Aggressors

Did you know that children and teens who bully have often been bullied themselves or been abused in some way at some point in their lives? It's even possible that a teen who is bullying is also being actively bullied at the same time. Here are some common signs someone may start or may already be engaged in bullying behavior:

- Having friendships with other teens known to bully
- Getting into physical fights frequently
- Engaging in aggressive acts at home or school
- Experiencing increasing disciplinary action in school (detention/suspension)
- Frequently blaming others for problems and actions
- Being preoccupied about their reputation or popularity

INTERVENING AND GETTING HELP

Unfortunately, many victims of bullying feel helpless and alone. These feelings make it difficult for a victim to seek help. Additionally, bullying typically involves intimidation, and victims often fear that speaking up will result in severe backlash — either from the bully or his or her peers. Further, many teens and kids try to mitigate the humiliation of being bullied by pretending everything is fine.

Obviously, it's not. If you are being bullied or know a friend or family member who is, the best thing you can do is to speak up! Believe it or not, bullying generally stops within seconds of someone intervening. That doesn't mean the bullying is over for good, but the person being bullied knows that someone cares, and the bully knows that someone else is paying attention.

Talk to an adult you trust — a parent, counselor, teacher, religious leader, or relative. This is a critical first step of getting help for yourself or someone else. This isn't about tattling; it's about potentially saving a life, either yours or someone you love's. A teacher or administrative staff member can help put a stop to bullying if it's happening at school or if it's happening online and involving schoolmates.

If you experience cyberbullying, *don't respond.* Don't forward the messages. Don't interact. Instead, block that person from social media immediately, and report inappropriate language, actions, or content to the platform through which the messages were sent. If cyberbullying involves schoolmates, also report it to a teacher or administrative staff member.

Cyberbullying isn't simply cruel and humiliating; it can be illegal. There may be instances when reporting it to law enforcement is necessary. If you or a friend ever receive online threats, pornographic photographs, secretly recorded videos, or content that could be construed as a hate crime, it needs to be reported to the police. Keep any messages or content you receive, as these will be critical in holding those who sent them accountable.

Bullies thrive when those around do nothing. Take action to help preserve the self-esteem, confidence, health, and perhaps even the life of someone you know.

Chapter 6

SELF-HARM

Everyone wants to bang their head against a wall in frustration sometimes, but most people don't actually do it. After all, hitting your head against a wall *hurts*. However, self-harm can actually become a coping mechanism (granted, an unhealthy one) for some people — particularly teens — who feel overwhelmed by frustration, depression, anxiety, trauma, or mental illness. For someone in deep emotional pain, self-harm does provide a kind of relief, but at a cost.

KALEY'S STORY

I grew up in Pennsylvania with divorced parents who lived in different states. My mother was a single mom who worked full time, and after school I usually ended up at my uncle's house. Because he lived just a few blocks away and worked nights, he was almost always home in the afternoon. When I was eleven or so, my uncle began molesting me. I was a child and didn't understand what was happening, and because my mother was always under a lot of stress, I didn't tell anyone about the abuse. It went on for several years; usually it happened only when my uncle was angry or drunk.

I became very quiet, shy, and withdrawn. I thought that if I could make my mother happy and my uncle happy, the abuse would stop, but it continued despite how I acted or what I did. After a few years, my mother got a new job in another town, and we moved away. By this time I was a teenager, and my mom still had no idea what had happened so many times at my uncle's house.

Even after I moved and the abuse stopped, I felt very alone. I would go over and over the events in my head and think about all the things I could have done differently that might have made it stop — or prevented it altogether. At times like these, I dug my fingernails into my skin so hard I bled. In a way, I felt I was punishing myself for all the actions I didn't take when I could have.

I tried to make friends, but I always felt isolated and different and never knew quite what to say. The loneliness made me depressed, and in school I was always wary and suspicious of adults — particularly male adults — and couldn't bring myself to open up to anyone.

One day when I was fifteen, I sat alone in my bedroom thinking about the abuse. I had a paper clip in my hand and slowly straightened it out so I had the point of it against the skin of my forearm. I pressed it into my skin hard, scraping it until I saw a small path of blood. It should have hurt, but I just felt relief. I focused on the stinging in my skin rather than all the thoughts running through my mind, and I felt better than I had in a long time.

Not long after, I walked into a hardware store after school and bought a package of razor blades. I kept these hidden in my desk at home, and when the thoughts and memories were too much for me to bear, I'd make a cut on my forearm. Sometimes the cuts were shallow scratches, sometimes deeper. Once I worried I might need stitches, but I didn't want anyone to find out about what I was doing.

I stopped wearing tank tops and even short sleeves. Even in the summer heat, I wore long-sleeve shirts to make sure no one saw my arms. One day when I was just out of the shower, my mother caught a glimpse of a fresh cut and forced me to show her my arms. She asked why I would do this to myself. I couldn't answer her. I didn't *know* why I did it. I just knew that it made me feel better.

My mom arranged for me to talk to a counselor. After several very quiet sessions, I finally told the counselor about the abuse. That was when she explained to *me* why I was cutting. I had experienced sexual abuse and continued to experience post-traumatic stress from those events.

Once I opened up about the abuse and began taking positive steps toward working through it, I realized that I didn't have the same urge to cut anymore. Of course, there were days — and still are — that were overwhelming, and all those feelings of guilt, shame, isolation, and pain would come flooding back. At those times, I sometimes found myself imagining how it would feel to cut again. Often this happened after an event or situation that reminded me of the time in my life I was being abused.

Working with a counselor, I was able to address the root cause of my cutting and the reason for my post-traumatic stress. Through her help, I became healthy enough to make new friends, and eventually I graduated from college and now have a successful, professional career. The scars of my past are still visible — literally — and I'm often still self-conscious of them. But those who are closest to me know what they're from and why they're there. To say that I'm the same person I was before I experienced the abuse would be untrue, but I'm a happy, healthy adult and have been able to make and maintain healthy relationships.

Self-harm isn't something I ever planned on doing, but my scars remind me of it every day. I don't want anyone reading this book to go through what I went through. I hope that teens reading this know that there are so many other outlets out there — your teachers, counselors, and parents, just to name a few. Even a close friend might be the person who helps you make a positive change. You're not alone, so please don't ever think there's nowhere else to turn.

WHAT IS SELF-HARM?

Everyone deals differently with overwhelming feelings and emotions. Some people get angry and lash out at others when they feel stressed, disappointed, or embarrassed. Others withdraw and isolate themselves. And some — particularly teens — turn to self-harm as a coping mechanism.

Self-harm, also called self-injury, is the act of hurting yourself to cope with emotions that seem too much to bear. On the surface, it might sound related to suicide — after all, that's the ultimate self-harm, right? Self-injury is actually a totally different animal. It's not about ending your life — *usually*. It's about finding an outlet for pain, shame, guilt, and any other overwhelming emotion. That said, one of the dangers of self-harm is that accidental death *can* occur.

Like many cutters, Kaley didn't understand why she was doing what she was doing. She simply knew that it made her feel better. Yet there are several reasons people engage in self-harm. For many, self-injury provides an emotional release when they have no other outlet. For others, the injury serves to interrupt the numbness or nothingness (often caused by depression) they feel on a daily basis. Sometimes, self-injury can be a subtle, even subconscious, cry for help, while in others it could be a way to feel a sense of control when everything else feels *out* of control.

Further, not everyone who practices self-harm does so in the same manner. Cutting is the most common form of self-injury (and is used 70 to 90 percent of the time), but people also engage in burning (15 to 35 percent of the time), pulling hair, skin picking, and hitting and head-banging (21 to 44 percent). Because self-injury is a coping strategy and not a manipulation tactic, those who practice it are often secretive about what they're doing. That means it can be even harder for them to get the help they need.

RISKS AND SIGNS OF SELF-HARM

By definition, self-injury is a risky behavior. First, there's always the chance that someone will cut too deep, hit too hard, or cause a serious infection or permanent injury. Second, self-injury is an unhealthy way to express feelings, thoughts, fears, and experiences. Aside from the physical effects of the injury — like bruises, scars, nerve damage, broken bones, hair loss, and other physical ailments — self-injury can result in serious psychological effects. People who practice self-injury often experience feelings of shame and guilt over their behavior, leading to lower self-esteem and depression. Self-injury can also be addictive, and like many addictions, it can become worse and worse until the behavior is a serious health risk.

Since the people who practice self-harm are usually secretive about the behavior, it can be tough to spot the warning signs. Here are some of the most common signs and symptoms of self-harm:

- Scars that can't be explained
- Bald spots (where the person has pulled out hair)
- Burns or marks on the skin
- Keeping around sharp objects — like pocketknives or razor blades
- Spending a lot of time alone
- Wearing long-sleeved clothing or long pants even on warm days
- Avoiding talking about feelings or expressing emotions

PREVALENCE OF AND RISK FACTORS FOR SELF-HARM

How many teens engage in self-harm? According to Teen Help, one-third to one-half of US adolescents have engaged in some kind of self-injury, and one in every two hundred girls aged thirteen to nineteen cut themselves regularly. According to the *American Journal of Public Health*, on average as many as one in four girls aged fourteen to eighteen self-injure every year, while on average one in ten teenage boys self-injure.

That doesn't mean that all teens are equally at risk, though preadolescents and teens are more likely to hurt themselves than other age groups. However, certain risk factors make some people much more likely to engage in self-harm. These include but are not limited to the following:

- A history of physical or sexual abuse
- Being an adolescent girl (which is the most common demographic for self-injury)
- A family history of self-injury
- Mental illness, including borderline personality disorder, bipolar, major depression, and anxiety disorders
- Alcohol and substance abuse
- A history of PTSD

As Kaley describes in her story, she was at serious risk for self-injury for several reasons. Not only was she an adolescent female, but she also had a history of sexual abuse, which led to post-traumatic stress disorder (PTSD) and depression. Kaley used self-injury as an outlet for the overwhelming emotions she was experiencing.

GENUINE COPING MEANS NO SECRETS

The other thing that Kaley's story illustrates is how self-harm can be used to mask the real issue. Like drugs and alcohol, self-injury might offer temporary relief or distraction, but it also exacerbates the underlying problems. Kaley only began to feel better in a lasting way when she confronted the main cause of her self-injury: the PTSD and depression caused by her sexual abuse.

In other words, self-harm does not solve someone's problems. In fact, it's often done in secret in order to avoid facing the underlying issues. If you or someone you know is practicing self-harm, the most important thing to do is to tell a trusted adult, so they can help you or the other person find healthy ways to cope. This isn't the time to keep secrets or to hide what is happening out of a sense of shame; self-injury is serious and can even be fatal when taken too far. The most important thing is to ask for and gather the caring support of others to help you through it.

Chapter 7

POST-TRAUMATIC STRESS DISORDER (PTSD)

When you hear the term *post-traumatic stress disorder*, or *PTSD*, what comes to mind? Is it soldiers returning from war or survivors of a mass shooting? Of course, those and other violent events can cause PTSD, but you don't have to survive a personal or violent attack in order to develop PTSD and for feelings of fear, stress, and pain to affect you for a long, long time.

In essence, whenever we encounter a scary situation, our brain experiences an instinctual fight-or-flight response: We either defend ourselves or attempt to get away and avoid the danger. This self-protective response is natural, and it usually ends or goes away when the danger is over. However, people with PTSD continue to feel that fight-or-flight response even when there's no actual danger present.

That said, everyone reacts to trauma differently, and what people experience as traumatic differs. Not every person with PTSD has lived through a horrific event, and not every person who *has* experienced trauma suffers from PTSD. Other situations — like the sudden loss of a loved one, childhood neglect, or any kind of abuse, whether one-time or ongoing — can also cause PTSD. Further, there's no predicting how long PTSD will last. Some recover after a matter of months, while others experience chronic and even lifelong PTSD symptoms. That's why, if you recognize any of the signs, it's important to seek professional help.

PTSD: SIGNS AND RISK FACTORS

PTSD is a disorder fueled by memories. The symptoms of PTSD are all about how your mind and body react to or re-call those memories. These symptoms include the following:

- Nightmares
- Flashbacks
- Denial or suppression of memories
- Depression
- Avoiding situations that trigger memories of the event
- Irritability or emotional outbursts
- Impulsive or aggressive behavior (more common in teens than young children)
- Insomnia
- Headaches
- Anxiety about possible danger (either real or imagined)
- Inability to get your mind off the event

Usually, symptoms of PTSD develop within about three months of the trauma, but like any mental disorder, every case is different. Sometimes PTSD doesn't occur until years after the event.

While any stressful or traumatic situation can result in PTSD — experiences like war, sexual abuse, being mugged, witnessing violence, or being in a car accident — there are several reasons someone might be at greater risk for developing it. These often relate to a previous history of difficult or traumatic experiences, which can include the following:

- **Neglect:** According to the National Center for PTSD, neglect is the leading cause of PTSD in children and young adults (65 percent).
- **A history of abuse:** Other common causes among children and teens include physical abuse (18 percent), sexual abuse (10 percent), and psychological abuse (7 percent).
- **Drug and alcohol abuse**
- **Lack of social support**
- **Witnessing family violence:** From three to ten million children witness family violence each year, and about 40 to 60 percent of those cases involve child abuse.
- **Being female:** While similar percentages of boys and girls experience at least one trauma (from 15 to 43 percent), of those, 3 to 15 percent of girls and 1 to 6 percent of boys develop PTSD.

In Kaley's story in chapter 6, she describes a history of sexual abuse and a lack of social support, and there's little doubt these factors played a role in Kaley's development of PTSD.

TREATING PTSD

Living with PTSD isn't something any teen should have to experience. Fortunately, as with other mental disorders, there's help available if you need it. Of course, the best thing to do if you suspect you have PTSD is to talk to a healthcare professional. If you don't feel comfortable doing that, talk to someone you trust, preferably an adult. Friends can be and are a great support system, but an adult is more likely to have the resources and know-how to get you the help you really need. If you don't want to talk to your parents, seek a school counselor, family doctor, clergy member, teacher, or even a trusted family friend, or contact an organization listed in the resources.

Don't wait. Like depression, PTSD is *treatable,* but without treatment, the symptoms tend to get worse. Deal with the symptoms now to avoid living through months or even years of continued trauma and stress. Remember Kaley: The first step to a genuinely happy, healthy self is to acknowledge and face what's difficult.

Chapter 8

PEER PRESSURE AND STRESS

According to the American Psychological Association's Stress in America survey, today's teens are more stressed out than adults. That's right! The next time you hear your mom or dad say, "I'm stressed," just tell them, "Well, I'm more stressed out than you!" Statistics back you up.

All joking aside, stress is a serious matter. As a teen, you have to deal with an enormous amount of pressure every single day. You have pressure to fit in and make friends while wanting to be accepted for who you are. Pressure to get good grades. Pressure to make the baseball team or debate team. Pressure to get into college. Pressure, perhaps, to try drugs or alcohol. Pressure to wear the right clothes or own the right gear. Depending on your home life, you could feel pressure to support a parent or sibling who is struggling, whether from divorce, mental illness, or medical problems.

Even if you are pretty chill and feel like you handle stress well, you're human, and all of these pressures have a cumulative effect on your well-being. Let's be honest — handling stress is sometimes a *big* effect.

PEER PRESSURE

Teens have a lot to figure out. They are still discovering who they are, and yet they must make big decisions without a lot of life experience. Many feel the pressure to choose a life's career by the time they graduate high school — before their brains have even finished developing! Teens are continually faced with decisions to try new things, to dance and date, to drink beer, to get a job, to drive, to have sex.

Like most teens, you probably have no shortage of people willing to help you make those decisions — from your parents to your teachers to your closest group of friends. The question is, who do you listen to? Another source of stress for teens is deciding who to let influence your life on a day-to-day, even a moment-to-moment, basis. Most teens, and in fact most people, are heavily influenced by their peers, those friends who share their circumstances and social circle.

The advice and influence of your peers can be a great thing. When your friends have your best interests in mind, they can guide and push you to make good choices, to take the right risks in order to grow and succeed. Your best friend might convince you to go out for track and field, and who knows? Running could become your passion for the rest of your life. We all need friends to help us discover and become our best selves.

But another truth is, sometimes a peer group can influence you to make decisions you really don't *want* to make just because you feel pressure to do it. That's what "peer pressure" refers to, negative influence or the dark side of this dynamic. Peer pressure is when you're influenced to do something you don't want, and the reasons can vary. Sometimes it may be to avoid feeling embarrassed or shameful; sometimes so that you fit in with everyone else; and sometimes friends might offer convincing reasons or just plain badger you until you give in. Many times, this negative peer pressure can influence you to try new experiences you're not ready to try or do things you know are inappropriate or wrong. When this happens, these experiences can have a major effect on your sense of self-worth and your mental health. Doing something for the wrong reasons — especially if you don't want to do that something at all — doesn't make you feel good about yourself. And as this book makes clear, low self-esteem can lead to depression, further risky behaviors, and even suicide.

PEER PRESSURE, SELF-ESTEEM, AND DEPRESSION

Giving in to peer pressure can eat away at someone's self-esteem. Unfortunately, low self-esteem also puts people more at risk of giving in to peer pressure. It's a vicious cycle.

When you lack confidence, you may already feel like you don't fit in, which can make it even more important to try — at any cost. Low self-esteem is that voice inside that tells us we're not good enough — not cool enough, not pretty enough, not smart enough. And when we feel like that, it's easy to give in to anything that might make us feel, well, *enough.*

Unfortunately, giving in to peer pressure and doing what you don't want usually has the opposite effect. Your self-esteem drops even more, which then — guess what? — makes you more likely to give in again, and again and again.

The crux of the problem is that, when you try to fit in by doing things you normally wouldn't, *you're not being yourself.* For teens who are already confused about who they are, this only adds to the confusion and discomfort. And over time, it also increases anxiety, since you know you're not being au-thentic and always risk being found out. This is a perfect rec-ipe for — you guessed it — developing depression.

Once someone becomes depressed, it becomes even harder to end the messy cycle of peer pressure: giving in to fit in, which leads to guilt and self-doubt, which makes the person feel even less part of the group, which makes them try even harder the next time. This is also why we some-times don't recognize someone who is struggling with peer pressure–related depression. From the outside, they might appear to be the opposite — the life of the party, the one who's always willing to say yes and impress others by taking risks. Sometimes people hide their struggles, which aren't obvious. There's more to people than they usually show. Always remember, there can be a lot hiding beneath the surface.

Peer Pressure Risk Factors

We *all* feel peer pressure, and we all let our peers influence our decisions now and then. But some people are more likely to give in to negative peer pressure just because of their background and life experiences. You might be more at risk for peer pressure if you experience the following:

- Low self-esteem
- Social uncertainty (you don't know where you fit in)
- A learning disability or poor academic performance
- Lack of confidence, particularly in social circles
- Lack of hobbies or interests
- Distrust of others
- Weak support system (lack of family support or healthy friendships)
- Insecurity about your appearance or economic background

ACADEMIC PRESSURE

I don't have to tell you high school isn't easy. You're living it. However, in addition to everything else going on, let's not overlook one key challenge of high school — the *school* part. How well you do academically can have a huge influence on your future — like where (or whether) you'll go to college, what you'll study, and what employment or life opportunities will be available for you. Because academic performance is so important, teens get overwhelmed by the pressure to succeed, which can have a negative impact on mental health.

If you're stressed about your academic performance, take heart. Most students around the world are. A 2015

Organisation for Economic Co-operation and Development study surveyed the well-being of teens in seventy-two different countries, and it found that 66 percent felt stressed about their grades and anxious about homework and tests. But when it comes to high school, academic pressure involves more than just grades. Most teens are involved in extracurricular activities of some kind, like sports, music, or drama. These might be causing stress if they get in the way of keeping grades up. Even teens who get good grades can become stressed if they aren't doing well enough — at least in comparison to siblings or friends, up to parental standards, or to get into their desired college. Whatever the reason, there can be a lot of pressure to "keep up."

Academic pressure is a heavy burden to bear — and I wish I could tell you that, once high school is over, all that pressure just melts away. Unfortunately, that's not the world we live in. You probably already know that — and *that* can also cause stress. You'll feel pressure in college, and you'll feel pressure to get a good job and "move up" in the professional world. Our society doesn't just applaud accomplishment — it *demands* it. You might wonder if it ever ends.

It doesn't. Which is why recognizing and coping with stress is such a vital life skill. When it comes to academic and professional success, one of the most important things is to learn not to let it affect your self-esteem and self-worth. Be proud of what you accomplish, but don't despair if you don't meet your goals. Just keep trying, and remember: Your self-worth comes from somewhere much deeper — from the fact that you are *you*. *No one*, and I mean *no one*, can compete with you on that.

RECOGNIZING STRESS

Just the word *stress* kind of stresses me out. But you know what? Stress is part of life, and sometimes it can actually be really helpful. Stress can be a great motivator to succeed — in *anything*. But too much stress is linked to a *lot* of bad stuff, from heart disease to obesity to anxiety and depression. Sometimes we don't even realize how stressed we are. So the question to ask is: Do you feel a "helpful" amount of stress, so that your desire to do well actually spurs you to achieve more, or is an "unhelpful" amount of stress undermining your efforts? Do you recognize any of these signs of too much stress?

- You have nervous habits, like drumming your fingers, biting your nails, or tapping your feet.
- You don't sit down for meals.
- You're late all the time.
- You keep forgetting appointments or events.
- You feel irritable or snap at friends and family.
- You don't hang out with friends as much as you used to.
- You get sick all the time.
- You have a hard time concentrating.
- You have a hard time falling or staying asleep.
- You consume too much caffeine.
- You always feel like you're "falling behind."

If high school has you feeling any of the above, you're probably too stressed. What can you do about it? First of all, relax and give yourself a break. When we fall behind or underachieve, we often think: *I need to work harder*. Well, guess what? When we're too stressed, working harder doesn't always help. In fact, it can do the opposite and make us more stressed. Think about it: If you're running a marathon and your body feels like it's going to give out, what do you do? Run harder and faster? Of course not; you ease up, pace yourself, and drink some water. You want to finish the race, even if you don't run as fast as you wanted, rather than collapse halfway through and not finish at all. The same idea is true when you're in an academic pressure cooker.

DEALING WITH PRESSURE AND STRESS

After many years dealing with stress of all kinds, I've found that my number-one stress reliever, hands down, is exercise. Exercise releases endorphins, powerful chemicals that help elevate your mood and even reduce pain (physically and mentally). I also find that meditation really helps me recenter, refocus, and calm my nerves. These might help you as well, but the important thing is to find out exactly what helps *you* deal with the stresses and pressures in your life. Here are a few tried-and-true methods:

- **A healthier diet:** Your physical body has a *huge* effect on your mental well-being. When you're getting the nutrients you need — including vitamins, electrolytes, proteins, and healthy fats — your brain is better equipped to process your to-do list and to focus on the task at hand.
- **Belief:** I think it's important to believe in *something* greater than ourselves. Focus on whatever that is for you — God, karma, the universe,

nature, a good cause, your family and friends, art or music, even sports. Working toward anything you love can help you feel centered and capable of greatness.

- **Outdoor activities:** I always make a strong case for exercise, but in fact, just *being* outside can be good for the soul. Nature is a natural (literally) stress-reliever. Get outdoors whenever possible.
- **Time with friends and family:** Your friends and family make up your primary support group. When we're stressed, we often isolate ourselves, which actually makes stress worse. Talk to your parents, siblings, or friends about what you're feeling. Even if they simply listen, talking is cathartic.
- **Professional therapy:** When life gets too tough, it's time to talk about it. A professional can help you deal in a healthy way with the pressure you feel.

Try one or more of these ideas, see which ones help you feel less stressed, and see chapter 14 for more lifestyle advice. What other healthy things can you think of that *aren't* in this list? Learning to cope with stress in a healthy manner is a skill you'll use your whole life.

Chapter 9

ANXIETY

Sweaty palms?

Rapid heartbeat?

Butterflies in your stomach?

Do any of these sound familiar? I promise you, you're not on a roller coaster, you're just experiencing a "normal" day of anxiety. A lot of people — especially teens — don't recognize anxiety as a problem because *everyone* gets anxious. I mean, I get jittery every time I step in front of a crowd of people — or speak to a classroom of students. You might get nervous before a test, sporting event, or performance. Anxiety is a natural part of life.

Except, like stress, when it becomes debilitating.

When anxiety becomes so frequent or pervasive that it interferes with your schoolwork, social life, or sleeping patterns, it needs to be addressed. Anxiety, like depression, is treatable, but many teens don't seek help because anxiety play tricks on your body and it plays tricks on your mind.

ASHER'S STORY

When I was four years old, I'd practice listening to my stuffed animals' heartbeats using a stethoscope my grandmother gave me for Christmas. I'd also wrap my dog's legs and head in gauze. I pretty much kept my entire family covered in bandages! I knew then that I wanted to be a doctor when I grew up.

In first grade, I proudly shared my medical aspirations with my teacher. She told me I'd have to get really, really good grades to get into medical school, and then work hard to actually become a doctor. But when it came to school and grades, I did terribly. Reading and writing were so confusing to me that I begged my parents to let me stay home.

By third grade, I still struggled reading an entire sentence. I was behind in everything at school and always in trouble because I was disruptive or wasn't paying attention. In fact, the only "subject" I was good at was art. I could focus for hours on painting or modeling clay, but I couldn't get through a simple picture book.

My parents took me to a learning disabilities specialist, who diagnosed me as severely dyslexic. I began going to special therapy sessions to help my reading and writing, but my progress was slow. It was so slow, in fact, that things at school only got worse.

Knowing I had a disability, the teacher treated me differently. That was fine, but the students all noticed. They'd tease me by holding up a page of a book and demanding that I read it out loud. When I ignored them, they called me "retard" and "dummy." By middle school, I hated school more than anything.

By high school, I had ways of dealing with the dyslexia, but I was increasingly anxious about anything academic.

These feelings were at their worst on test days, when I knew I'd have to "perform" within a constricted amount of time. I pretended to be sick or even skipped school altogether on test days. I also hated choir on the days it involved reading new music.

My parents continued paying a learning therapist to tutor me once a week. This helped, but I felt guilty all the time. I knew money was tight for them and the therapist was a big expense. Plus, I didn't feel like I was getting better fast enough. I felt so much pressure to improve and to *finally* get an A — or at least a C+ — in English or history. But my grades continued to be mediocre, and I felt like a burden on my parents.

Every morning I tried to *want* to go to school. But I just couldn't. School made me so nervous and anxious that sometimes I even vomited on my way there. Because I felt so different, I didn't make friends easily and ended up feeling lonely and isolated on top of everything else. At this point I knew I would never be a doctor. I didn't even know if I'd graduate high school.

With therapy, my reading improved. But that didn't matter as much anymore. I was so anxious about school that I still couldn't concentrate in class — *if* I made it to class at all. By the end of my junior year, I was told I'd have to repeat the grade again because I'd had so many absences.

This devastated my parents, who thought the expensive therapy was working — and it was. What they didn't know was that I was suffering from debilitating anxiety. Even if I'd prepared for a quiz, I still felt physically unable to get myself into the classroom to take it. I wanted to hide from my peers who called me dumb, the teachers who treated me like I was broken, and my parents who kept sacrificing for me, even though my grades weren't improving.

One morning before school, I experienced an actual panic attack. Of course, I didn't know that was what it was at the time. My heart was beating out of my chest. I was sweaty and dizzy and felt like I couldn't breathe. I was sure I was going to die. My mother rushed me to the emergency room, and the doctor, after an examination and a dose of medication, referred me to a psychiatrist, who diagnosed me with anxiety and prescribed more therapy.

I was glad to have an explanation for what I was experiencing, but I felt really guilty adding *more* therapy and doctor visits to my parents' stretched budget. When I got up the courage to share with my mom, she looked at me, took my face in her hands, and said, "There's nothing more important to us than your happiness. I'm so sorry you've felt like this for so long." It felt like a ton of bricks had been lifted from my shoulders.

School has never gotten "easy" for me, but with therapy and medication, I'm confident I can manage it. I *did* graduate from high school, and I'm currently enrolled in a junior college. Honestly, I don't know if I'll ever be the doctor I dreamed I'd be. But I feel more capable today than I ever have, and I'm hopeful there are other dreams out there for me to pursue. I've also made a small circle of good friends. I hope to transfer to a four-year university soon and take a few premed courses to see how I do. With therapy, I've learned not to put so much pressure on myself.

I still get anxious sometimes, but I've found better ways to cope so that I don't get nearly as stressed out about it. When I think about it, that panic attack was a turning point, and it actually kind of saved my life. I knew

I had a learning disability, but before that day I never grasped what was *really* going on in my brain. I'm also glad now that I got help before things continued to spiral downward.

My anxiety didn't let me really see the world around me. It turns out the world around me is pretty awesome, and most days I'm excited to be in it. And on the days when I'm not, I know the healthy actions I can take to feel better. Slowly, I'm starting to see how anything is possible.

ANXIETY SYMPTOMS AND RISK FACTORS

What does anxiety feel like? Everyone experiences anxiety differently. For some, anxiety might be the constant feeling that something is going to go wrong. For others, it could be an irrational, inexplicable fear. Anxiety often feels like you're really worried about something — but you might not even be able to pinpoint *what* that something is. People suffering from anxiety also often have physical symptoms ranging from insomnia to stomachaches, headaches, and even hyperventilation. You might have anxiety if any of the following sound familiar:

- You avoid activities you used to love, out of fear or worry.
- You frequently feel like something bad is going to happen.
- You're so worried that you have trouble sleeping.
- Your heart beats fast (for no reason) frequently.
- At times, you're short of breath or it's hard to breathe (when you're not exercising).
- You have sore muscles or your body feels tense.

- You feel weak and lethargic.
- You frequently have stomachaches.
- You sweat more than normal.
- You get obsessed about certain things.
- You avoid certain situations, locations, or even thoughts due to fear.

Anxiety is a part of life, and many of us feel anxious to a certain degree in various situations. Anxiety becomes a problem when it interferes with your life or makes you "feel crazy." Panic attacks are when anxiety comes in fast, strong waves without any warning. If you've never experienced one, it can be really scary. When you're having a panic attack, you could experience some or all of these symptoms:

- Rapid heartbeat or actual heart palpitations
- Chest pain
- Shortness of breath or feeling like you can't breathe
- Fear that you're having a heart attack or dying
- Extreme nausea
- Uncontrolled shaking
- Feelings of suffocation
- Dizziness
- Hot flashes or sweating

Panic attacks are serious business. In fact, many people who experience one seek emergency help because the sensation of dying feels so *real*. That's the thing about anxiety disorders and other mental illnesses. They skew your reality — to the point that you experience genuine, physical symptoms.

Someone suffering from an anxiety disorder doesn't just feel too stressed or nervous to concentrate sometimes. They feel scared, nervous, panicked, and uneasy all the time, and tasks that should be easy or manageable become really hard to do. To call anxiety a mental illness doesn't mean it doesn't create real, physical symptoms and real problems in someone's life. When you suffer from anxiety, you might experience any of these issues:

- Problems with your school performance, or even dropping out of school
- Loss of friends
- Low self-esteem
- Reckless or impulsive behaviors
- "Missing out" on events or hobbies you once enjoyed

It's also important to understand that if you suffer from an anxiety disorder, you're much more likely to abuse drugs or alcohol. Usually, that's a sign that you're self-medicating in order to calm the feelings brought on by anxiety. While these substances might offer short-term relief, they worsen symptoms exponentially in the long term.

TYPES OF ANXIETY DISORDERS

A number of disorders and phobias fall under the umbrella of anxiety. Anxiety can be generalized, and often is, but it can also express itself in very specific ways. Here are some of the more common types:

- **Generalized anxiety disorder (GAD):** This is the most commonly diagnosed anxiety disorder.

People suffering from GAD worry about everyday things — from work to family to finances —
to the point that these worries interfere with
daily life and responsibilities.

- **Panic disorder:** Panic attacks can happen with
  any anxiety disorder. What differentiates panic
  disorder from other issues like PTSD (which
  frequently causes panic attacks) is the absence
  of an underlying trauma. In fact, for someone
  suffering from panic disorder, the panic attacks
  themselves can *become* a trauma that causes or
  exacerbates other symptoms of anxiety.

- **Obsessive-compulsive disorder (OCD):** While
  people frequently joke about being "OCD," most
  are not. This disorder is genuinely debilitating
  and even frightening to those who suffer from
  it. People with OCD feel compelled to repeat
  behaviors or actions, obsessing on those actions
  until they find relief by performing them.

- **Separation disorder:** It's normal to have anxiety
  about leaving home or being away from family or
  friends. Separation disorder describes feeling so
  much distress and anxiety over separation (from
  certain people or a place) that it interferes with
  everyday life and makes it difficult to function.

- **Social phobia (agoraphobia):** Not everyone is
  a *people person*, but those with agoraphobia experience genuine fear or even panic in certain
  public places or situations. People with social
  phobia may go to great lengths to avoid public

events, parties, certain open or enclosed spaces, and crowds of people.

Keep in mind that your risk of having *any* anxiety disorder is increased if you have a family history of anxiety, have experienced a trauma, or abuse drugs and alcohol. And since anxiety disorders often come in packs, if you suffer from one, you may be at greater risk of experiencing others. If you think you may have an anxiety disorder, it's time to talk about it! A mental health professional can help you get a proper diagnosis as well as treatment and therapy, so you can cope with the symptoms and manage your day-to-day life better. Recognizing anxiety is the first step to dealing with it.

Chapter 10

SUBSTANCE ABUSE

All of us are a work in progress, but teens are in a development phase *full time*. That's a big deal, and it can be exhausting — both physically and emotionally. When teens throw powerful substances like drugs, alcohol, cigarettes, or steroids into the mix, it can have a huge impact on their development — and not in a good way.

CONNOR'S STORY

Thirteen sounds young to me now, but when I was a newly minted teenager, just barely thirteen, I was sure I was invincible. I definitely felt that way when I was smoking. Well, actually there was no smoke involved. My friends and I loved vaping, and we'd spend our afternoons after school doing it — in the park or at one of our homes if our parents were gone. When you're thirteen, vaping feels really cool, and since our e-cigarettes were nicotine-free, I thought it was totally safe. Unfortunately, I didn't know then how harmful vaping really is — for several reasons. Not only do e-cigarettes contain harmful chemicals I knew *nothing* about, but they were also the first step for me into a spiral of addiction that nearly took my life.

Alcohol was an obvious choice when we were ready for something more exciting than vaping. My parents threw parties all the time, and they had a huge supply of liquor — every kind you could imagine. Because they entertained so often, they didn't notice when a bottle or two disappeared. The first time we tried it we shared a bottle of scotch, which I thought was disgusting. But before long, I was feeling light and floaty, and even though it burned going down my throat, I wanted more.

Alcohol was almost too convenient. Whether we swiped it from our parents' collection or paid our older siblings to buy it for us, we could get buzzed just about any night of the week. None of us were old enough to drive, so we never had to worry about getting hurt — back then I thought that was the only way drinking could hurt you.

Once, while I was with my friends, vaping and drinking beer, my buddy's older brother took some weed out of his backpack. I had a hard time inhaling the smoke at first, but once I did, I loved being stoned. We'd go to parties, drink alcohol, smoke pot, and meet new people who did the same. It seemed like anytime I met a new group of friends, they'd eventually introduce me to a new drug. Even though I wasn't even sixteen years old and lived in a suburban neighborhood, I was surprised at the variety of substances around to try. Plus, the parties we hit were so much cooler than the high school dances or football games other kids my age went to. In fact, there were usually older people there, too — college kids with access to awesome stuff I'd never tried.

One of those things was Percocet. I'd had it once, when my friend swiped a couple of pills from his grandmother's medicine cabinet. I barely remember it because it was so strong, and I wasn't used to being high yet, but this time it was different. I remember thinking I never want to live without this stuff. I called the guy and asked if I could buy more. He said he didn't have any but knew someone who did. From then on, I was doing everything I could to get my hands on oxy — or oxycodone. I'd swipe bills from my parents' wallets or pawn stuff off I didn't think my parents would miss. Once I'd had a taste of opioids, it seemed like it'd be impossible to go back. On days I didn't use, I felt agitated and depressed — like I was trapped in my own body. All day I'd look forward to when I could take a pill. Sometimes, if I was especially stressed, I'd take two after school or even one while I was *at* school.

After a few months, I called my contact and the line was out of service. I freaked out. I didn't know what I was going to do if I couldn't score more oxy. I went to a party where I knew there'd be heavy users and asked around. Someone told me I should just buy heroin. It was cheaper and much easier to get. It made sense. Heroin was something I could count on getting, even if my dealer disappeared. I bought some that night and shot up for the first time. It felt like I was always meant to shoot up.

What I didn't know then was that heroin is often cut with fentanyl, which is fifty times more potent than even heroin. I was using one of the most addictive substances around and felt like it was no big deal. I was only seventeen and had track marks on my arms. By this point there was no point hiding it, either. My parents kicked me out when I was sixteen when I came home from a stint in rehab, scored some meth, and got high in my room. High school was long over for me, of course.

But I had my friends to look out for me, or so I thought. We could get Narcan pretty easily, and this reverses the effects of an overdose. There was nothing worse than not shooting up enough heroin and having a dull or almost no high. Narcan let me shoot up what I wanted without fearing for my life — although I should have been fearing for my life, anyway. I figured the only way I was really in trouble was if I shot up alone. I was so, so wrong. My friends were like me: Nothing, *nothing* was more important than the drug. Without a fix, I literally felt like I was dying. I'd do anything to score again. I stole anything I could get my hands on. I did things I'm too ashamed to own. And after all that, I was still lucky. My last overdose landed me in the ER rather than a cemetery.

Unconscious in the hospital, I wasn't even expected to make it. Somehow the police found my parents, and when I woke up, they were there. My mom looked like she hadn't slept in years. My dad was crying. I was not even nineteen years old, but I'd given up my childhood completely. I gave up high school dances, graduation, family Christmases, and vacations. I didn't even notice when my birthday came and went that last year. I was dealing with hepatitis C, permanent damage to my brain and liver, and on top of all that, I'd shattered the lives of the people who loved me most. I didn't know if I'd ever recover from this — or if I even wanted to. My arms were permanently scarred from shooting up. No matter how long I lived, people who saw them would automatically assume I was a junkie.

If it weren't for my parents, I'd be dead. Not only did they do the right thing when they kicked me out of the house, they were the only people there for me when I was rushed to the ER as I was dying. I knew I had to either die or stop hurting them. They gave me the strength to stick with rehab. They forgave all the horrible things I'd done.

I know I'll always regret my teenage years, but I'm trying to make up for it now. I've earned my GED and am taking classes at a local community college until I can get into a four-year program. I attend Narcotics Anonymous meetings weekly because I know this addiction is never going to go away. If I could say anything to my younger self, or more importantly, to *you*, it's this: You're *not* invincible. You may think you know what you're taking, but you don't. Anything you buy or get is likely laced with various chemicals that will slowly — or quickly — damage your body and mind. As I said before, I was convinced e-cigarettes were safe because they didn't contain nicotine. Now I know that vaping devices contain chemicals linked to cancer and other diseases — and can set the stage for a lifetime of addiction problems. Taking that pill or smoking that pipe might feel like a fun thing to do, but you're just slowly surrendering your right and ability to make your own decisions. You're letting that drug own you, and it will keep owning you until it kills you.

Live your life the way *you* decide to live it. It seems so silly now that my teenage self never wanted to be bossed around or told what to do, only to give up my free will to dealers and packets of substances. Your future is bright. Don't let a drug decide it for you.

EXPERIMENTATION AND ADDICTION

Your teenage years are a time of discovery. You're exploring new experiences, new hobbies, and new relationships.

That curiosity can often include experimenting with behaviors that may be considered unhealthy or risky, at least when those behaviors are taken to an extreme. Of course, underage drinking, smoking, and drug use are illegal, but putting that aside, alcohol and cigarettes are not themselves illegal substances, and marijuana has been legalized in numerous places. Trying these doesn't necessarily indicate a substance-abuse problem, so long as you're smart and safe. Only you know what you've already tried, or what you'd like to try, and I'm not here to tell you what you should or should not do. It's likely you have parents, counselors, and other adults to help guide those decisions.

However, I've written this book to help you be the happiest, healthiest person you can be. And one thing that has been scientifically proven is that regularly consuming alcohol and/or using drugs increases the risk for depression and suicidal thinking and behavior. As I've already discussed, depression and mental disorders are the leading cause of suicide in the United States. You might be surprised to know that substance abuse is a close second.

By their very nature, alcohol and drugs interfere with your brain chemistry. Using these substances too often leads to misusing them, which can bring on serious depression. How much is too much? That depends on each person. People who already have a tendency toward depression because of their biology, family history, or other life stressors are at greater risk.

Many people who regularly "enjoy" alcohol or drugs are seeking an escape — maybe even from depression or another mental disorder. Since these substances can actually intensify depression, that can trap people in a vicious cycle with catastrophic consequences. The more someone "escapes" with drinking or drugs, the more depressed they become, and so the more they use until they become addicted, at which point it's hard to stop even when you try.

In fact, alcohol and drug abuse is common among teens. Curiosity plays a role, but so do peer pressure, stress, and mental and emotional issues. Of course, not every teen who takes a drink or tries pot becomes an addict. However, most adults who *are* addicts began using as teenagers. The Partnership for Drug-Free Kids reports that 90 percent of addictions begin in the teen years.

Addiction is terrifying. As Connor describes, addiction takes over your life, slowly robbing you of your self-esteem, your clear mind, and your ability to make your own decisions. As a teenager, you may not know whether you're genetically predisposed to substance abuse and addiction. To help assess your risk, talk to your parents about whether there's a family history of alcoholism or drug abuse. Also, know yourself. Do you already struggle with mental health issues that might make you susceptible to addiction — like ADHD, depression, anxiety, PTSD, bipolar disorder, and so on? If you drink or use regularly, look at yourself in the mirror: Do you show any of the warning signs below?

WARNING SIGNS OF SUBSTANCE ABUSE

Alcohol and drugs affect your brain, your emotions, and your behavior. In a way, that's why people take them; they don't want to feel "normal." But that's also what makes them dangerous. Alcohol and drugs interfere with your ability to assess risk, to make good choices, and to think of solutions to problems. It's not coincidental that people attempting suicide are often under the influence of alcohol or drugs.

Basically, alcohol and drugs turn you into *not you*. As they become addicting, alcohol and drugs have the power to alter every aspect of someone's life and personality: their physical health, their appearance, their moods, their grades, their friends, their judgment. If you already know someone with a problem, then you've likely seen these changes. Either way, here are the physical and behavioral signs of someone struggling with substance abuse.

Physical Warning Signs of Substance Abuse

- Bloodshot eyes
- Pupils that are larger or smaller than normal
- Frequent nosebleeds (could be caused by snorted drugs)
- Seizures
- Slurred speech
- Lack of personal hygiene
- Changes in appetite (weight gain or loss)
- Changes in sleep patterns
- Bruises or frequent injuries with no explanation
- Shakes or tremors

Behavioral Warning Signs of Substance Abuse

- Mood swings
- Deterioration of academic performance

- New or different friends, or isolation from long-time friends
- Apathy about interests or hobbies that were once important
- Poor concentration and poor memory
- Presence of alcohol or drug paraphernalia (bongs, shot glasses, and so on)
- Frequent fights or clashes with family members
- Sudden demand for privacy
- Theft of money, valuables, or prescription drugs
- Unusual hyperactivity, anxiety, or agitation

STEROID USE

I have firsthand experience with the dramatic effects of substance abuse. My husband, Bill, used steroids for much of his life. This abuse had a dramatic effect on his mood, temperament, and happiness, and it significantly contributed to his suicide. While less common in teens than in young adults, using performance-enhancing drugs during your adolescence is dangerous because these substances can greatly affect your hormonal system and your overall brain development. In fact, studies have indicated that steroid use can permanently alter your brain. Here's how to tell if someone is using steroids:

Physical Warning Signs of Steroid Use

- Testicular atrophy (the testes diminish in size)
- Acne (on the back, shoulders, face)
- Fast muscle growth, rapid weight gain

- Greasy hair, oily skin
- Increased breast tissue (especially in men)
- Bad breath
- Hair loss
- Joint pain
- Yellowing of skin
- Disrupted sleep
- Bloating and night sweats
- Nausea and vomiting

Behavioral Warning Signs of Steroid Use

- Mood swings, irritability, hyperactivity
- Verbal or physical abuse, aggression
- Feelings of invincibility
- Poor decision-making
- Secretiveness, lying, stealing
- Depression, lethargy (napping)
- Withdrawal from family members (locked bedroom door)
- Paranoia, hallucinations

It may sound corny, but I've always loved a little saying by Dr. Seuss: "Today you are you. That is truer than true. There's no one alive who is youer than you." Alcohol and drugs take the "you" away from you. Don't deprive the world of all the "you" you have to give by handing it over to a substance.

Chapter 11

TECHNOLOGY ADDICTION

Have you ever felt like you've lost time when perusing social media, playing video games, or watching YouTube? What happens when you start to crave — then *need* — that feeling of connectivity?

ETHAN'S STORY

If I could have, I think I would have wasted my entire life playing games online. My story started so innocently; I wasn't experimenting with drugs or being bullied at school. I just really liked playing video games. Growing up it was something I got to do after my homework was finished or on the weekends. But during my freshman year of high school, gaming wasn't just a hobby. In fact, my obsession with it became a huge problem. I didn't know it then, but my mental health was paying a huge toll for all the time I spent in a virtual reality.

When I was in the eighth grade, my parents got divorced. It was a tough time, but I knew I wasn't different than most of the kids I knew with divorced parents. My mom took a job in a town an hour away, and during the week I lived with my dad and grandma so I wouldn't have to change schools. Grandma's health wasn't great, and my dad worked long hours and often wouldn't get home until after dinner. Because of that, it seemed like I spent most of my time alone. That was fine because I wasn't super social. I tolerated school but didn't have close friends. I always felt a bit like an outsider. When I'd get home from school, I'd play video games, and for a couple of hours at least, I didn't think about my mom being gone, my dad working late, grandma's health getting worse, or the fact that I didn't really have anyone I could connect with.

The year I turned fifteen, there was an online video game that was so popular everyone was talking about it. When I tried it out, I was hooked immediately. Kids all over the world were playing this game, some of them on my own team, and we could talk to each other and help each other, even tell each other about our real lives — not that I had much of one anymore.

The more I played the game, the more I felt I had to play the game. I'd come home from school, skip my home-work, and go straight to my laptop. Sometimes I'd play so long I never actually made it into bed. I started feeling "sick" once a week or so because I was either too tired to go to school or I just wanted to play the game.

The game was technically free, but there were lots of cool weapons you could buy or features you could unlock with a credit card. I didn't have much money of my own — my dad gave me a little cash for lunch every week — but I didn't want to miss out on all the cool things my video game friends were buying. One night, while my grandma was asleep, I took a credit card from her wallet and saved the number to my gaming account. For a couple of weeks

I used the card to buy all kinds of things to make the game more fun. Then my grandma noticed and told my dad. As a punishment he took my laptop away for two weeks. Honestly, I wanted to die. I was so angry, but not just angry. I was depressed. I didn't know what to do with myself if I didn't have my laptop. I didn't have real friends to call or hang out with. I didn't know how to just get in bed and fall asleep. I wasn't interested in schoolwork or extracurricular activities.

Then the principal called my dad for a parent-teacher conference. On top of everything else, I was failing my classes. I didn't care about my homework, and I often didn't show up to school on test days. It didn't look likely that I'd even pass the ninth grade.

My dad called my mom after the conference, and I found out later they were both really worried. Dad told Mom that since he took my laptop away, I'd been angry and resentful, hadn't left my room, and wouldn't even come out for dinner. He had been worried about how much time I was spending online, and now he was worried about how depressed I was *without* spending time online.

My parents came to a decision together about what to do: I was only allowed to game for two hours each week-end day — *nothing* during the week. They told me they'd take my laptop and my phone when my two hours were up. I couldn't game during the week because they wanted me to focus on schoolwork and spend free time outside. If I didn't pull my grades up, I would lose even those four weekend hours. I was *furious*. I told them I hated them, that I'd never forgive them, and that I had no intention of doing homework or finding other hobbies.

I spent several weeks angry and resentful. Eventually, though, I started to feel better. It seemed like the less time I spent in front of my computer screen, the easier it was to be away from it. Not only that, but I just felt happier, lighter. I realized I *did* care about my grades, and I was even interested in my classes. Instead of sitting in front of my computer every evening and all weekend, I started running. Running helped me clear my mind and feel more positive. I'd run farther and farther until, eventually, I was running ten miles every weekend morning. Even though I was nervous about it, I joined my school's cross-country team. It turned out I was pretty good — and I *liked* the other kids on the team. For the first time maybe ever, I had a couple of good friends.

It seems like a little thing, but when my parents stepped in and set rules about the time I spent on my laptop, they really changed my life. If it'd been up to me, I'd have given up everything — even a high school diploma — for more time online. Even though I was angry for what seemed like a long time, I've actually thanked my parents several times for caring enough to do it. Today I'm in my senior year, and my GPA is 3.5. I'm applying to colleges, and I feel really positive about where my future leads. My parents "allow" an hour of gaming a day, but honestly, I rarely do it. I know firsthand what happens when technology becomes an addiction, and I don't want to go back to that place. If I could tell other teens one thing, I'd tell them to be open to your parents' "stupid" rules. When you're depressed or addicted to something, it's hard to see clearly. Fortunately, you probably have someone who loves you enough to see clearly *for* you — just like I did. Don't ever resent that.

TECHNOLOGY ON THE BRAIN

Question: At this moment, how far away is your phone?

Okay, that's kind of a rhetorical question. I spend a lot of time in high schools and a lot of time talking to teens, so

I know how important that device is. I'm guessing it's comfortably within arm's reach.

Smartphones aren't just for calling people — in fact, that's become a secondary (and sometimes all but *obsolete*) function of these magical devices. A smartphone holds our schedules and calendars, our music collection, photo archive, social media accounts, email, games, videos, even books. We use it to access the internet, communicate, and get work done. Considering everything our devices can do, it's no wonder they're rarely out of sight (or out of hand).

In fact, you might not be very surprised to learn that, according to a 2018 Pew Research report, 95 percent of US teens have access to a smartphone, and 45 percent claim they are online "almost constantly." That doesn't necessarily reflect addiction; smartphones and other devices are now an integral part of everyday life for many people of all ages. And yet, from the perspective of history, the current generation of teens is engaged in a society-wide technological experiment. No other generation has used technology this much. When I was your age, smartphones didn't exist, and no teens had cell phones. A "phone" meant a landline that served one function: making phone calls. If you weren't home, *people couldn't reach you.* (I know, right?)

So it's worth considering how smartphones affect you, and all teens, on a daily basis. Research shows that it isn't wholly positive. Teens today are more depressed than other generations, and they're more likely to attempt or complete suicide. And these rates of depression and suicide have increased dramatically since 2012, correlating with a surge in smartphone adoption by teens. This isn't coincidental. According to one 2018 study, teens who spent more hours on a smartphone, computer, or other device each day increased their risk for depression, anxiety, suicide, and suicidal behaviors. Of course, the solution sounds easy — spend *less* time on your device — but for some people that's *really* hard because technology addiction is real.

Technology and Addiction

When we hear the word *addiction*, we tend to think of substances like drugs, alcohol, and cigarettes — maybe even coffee and sugar — that provide our brains with stimulation and euphoria or with numbness and escape from pain. That little electronic device in your pocket and the big one on your desk can do the exact same thing: make the brain endlessly amused, stimulated, and relieved of worries and problems.

Technology can provide a high or an escape that's just as addicting as a drug and that works the same way. For some, social media provides little bursts of stimulation and validation that make them feel better. Someone who feels shy and misunderstood in person can go online and feel connected, understood, and outgoing. Or, like Ethan, someone might play video games to slip from reality — since playing numbs any stressful and painful feelings and replaces boredom with excitement.

Like any drug, once you start depending on the stimulation, it can be really difficult to go without it. Technology addiction is a vicious cycle, like all addiction, because the more you use it, the greater the risk of feeling depressed — and the more depressed you feel, the more you'll crave technology to make you feel better. And when your device is always within arm's reach, then you're just a video game, social media post, online purchase, text, or Snapchat away from a little relief. But like a drug-induced high, that relief is always temporary.

TECHNOLOGY ADDICTION SIGNS AND SYMPTOMS

Recognizing addiction is the critical first step in making the changes that will inevitably make you healthier and happier. Ask yourself these questions:

- Are you using your device more often than you used to?
- Do you ever feel like you've lost time playing games or spending time online?
- Do you feel anxious or uncomfortable when disconnected from your device?
- Do you pick up your device compulsively?
- Do your friends or family complain that you're always staring at your device?

Technology addiction is a tricky thing because, unlike a substance addiction, it can be difficult — or even impossible — to simply quit the "drug." Technology is a big part of our daily lives, and avoiding it is practically impossible. But when moderation turns into obsession, your mental health is likely to suffer. In fact, those with a technology addiction may exhibit or are at risk for the following:

- Sleep disorders due to staying up late or all night to use technology
- Weight gain or adverse health effects due to lack of physical exertion

- Social anxiety or difficulty with in-person inter-actions
- Irritability, anxiety, or anger when technology is disconnected
- Difficulty dealing with environmental or sched-ule changes that interfere with technology use
- Vision issues, including eye strain or discomfort
- Injuries due to using devices while walking or driving
- Low self-confidence, depression, and anxiety
- Frequent or constant feelings of dissatisfaction
- Substance abuse or dependence

Finally, teens addicted to technology are more likely to be-come addicted to substances. When someone uses technol-ogy like a drug, using drugs becomes just another method for feeling that same momentary pleasure and relief.

PRACTICE MODERATION: AVOIDING TECHNOLOGY ADDICTION

Once an addiction takes hold, it can be very hard and pain-ful to break it, as Ethan shares. If you suspect you're depend-ing on your device more than is healthy, and might be at risk for addiction, act now to practice moderation. This, in itself, can be difficult with technology. Unlike alcohol or cigarettes (or most drugs), which you don't need in order to live, you can't stop using computers and phones. Not in today's world. Living without technology is an unrealistic — perhaps impossible — goal. So here are several ways to curb usage and manage cravings.

Avoid "Idle" Technology Use

Think about when and why you most often reach for your phone. Chances are, it's during the "idle" moments of your day: between school periods, waiting for the bus, after you get home from school but before homework or chores, waiting for dinner, after going to bed but before turning off the light. In these moments, rather than reaching for a device, do something else to satisfy the craving for stimulation. You could even make a list: Listen to a favorite song, call a friend (yes, use your phone as an *actual phone!*), write a letter to a friend, organize your backpack or purse, read a book...you get the idea. If you touch the home button to avoid being bored, put the phone away.

Assess Your Usage

Have you ever heard the saying that you can't improve what you can't measure? Most devices provide information on how much time you're spending on it — and *how* you're spending that time. Review this. Quantify how much you're using technology. This can empower you to make healthy changes and allow you to measure the changes you make, like tracking weight loss during a diet. As you manage your usage and set limits for yourself, you'll know just how much of your time — and your life — are being spent in front of a screen.

Leave It Behind

I want to assure you it's possible to leave your phone at home and *not die*. In fact, spending time without your device can feel freeing. You're not controlled by (and can't give in to) the impulse to keep up. As you know, with technology you can *never* keep up. If you can't bring yourself to disconnect completely, try turning off your notifications so you only receive actual phone calls. If necessary, let parents and others know that you do this, so they know to call if something is important.

Put It to Bed

One major way technology addiction affects mental health is by depriving us of sleep. Sleep is critical to feeling healthy, both physically and mentally. If you only commit to one moderation strategy, make it this: *Turn off your phone before bed*. The blue light from your device has been shown to keep your brain awake, and it's so easy to get sucked into the technological vortex of online games, social media, and YouTube videos. Starting each day physically and mentally exhausted from lack of sleep makes everything else harder.

Talk to Someone

Hopefully, you're starting to see a theme in this book. Mental health issues are difficult to bear alone. That's why I continually urge you to talk to someone if you feel lost or out of control. Start with any adult you trust — a parent, counselor, teacher, clergy member, or family friend — and be honest about how you're feeling. If you're daunted at the thought of bearing something alone, *don't*. Your mental health is too important.

Chapter 12

SUICIDE

Most teens, after making a suicide attempt, say they did it to escape from a situation that seemed impossible to deal with or to get relief from bad thoughts or feelings. In this book, you've read stories from several teens who found themselves in exactly that type of situation — whether due to choices they made or a situation they couldn't control.

Most teens who attempt suicide don't necessarily want to die. They want to escape what's going on in their lives. And at that particular moment, dying seems like the only way out.

Some people who end their lives or attempt suicide might be trying to escape feelings of rejection, hurt, or loss. Others feel angry, ashamed, or guilty. Some may feel like a disappointment to friends or family. Others may feel unwanted, unloved, bullied, abused, or a burden to others.

In fact, everyone feels overwhelmed by difficult situations and emotions at times. *Everyone* is challenged to get through these experiences and find ways to carry on with determination and hope.

So why does one person try suicide when another in a similar situation does not?

Why are some people less resilient than others?

What convinces a person that the only way out of a bad situation is to end their life?

One answer is that most people who complete suicide have *depression*.

A LIFESAVING CONVERSATION

Do the following instructions sound familiar? Your parents have probably said these things before:

"Don't meet strangers online."
"Don't stay out after dark."
"Please don't text and drive."
"Don't do drugs."

But guess what? Most parents never talk about suicide. Let's face it — suicide is really sad, and it's uncomfortable. A lot of people don't know what to say or how to approach the topic of suicide, so instead they say or do nothing at all. However, teenagers are statistically more at risk of dying from suicide than from cancer, the flu, lung disease, heart disease, AIDS, pneumonia, and birth defects *combined*.

So it's time to start the conversation. And that conversation begins with *you* and some common myths.

Myths about Teen Suicide

As you read some of the myths about teen suicide (and the truth behind them), consider if you've heard any before. Has anyone, friend or family, used one to explain or dismiss someone's behavior or to avoid talking about suicide?

MYTH: Teens who threaten to complete suicide are just looking for attention.

This is not true. A teen talking about suicide should be taken seriously. In fact, teens tend to hide painful feelings and actions, like self-harm, so if someone you know has mentioned suicide, tell an adult you trust immediately.

MYTH: Asking teens if they've had thoughts about suicide increases their risk.

This is not true. Parents sometimes fear that bringing up the subject of suicide will somehow plant the seed to complete the act. In fact, the opposite is true. Addressing painful subjects like suicidal thoughts creates a safe space and a sense of relief for the individual having those thoughts, since he or she realizes someone cares and that help is available.

MYTH: Teens who aren't successful in completing suicide weren't serious.

This is not true. A teen who attempts suicide is trying to end his or her pain and suffering and is at a much higher risk of trying again. Second attempts at suicide are more likely to be lethal.

MYTH: Teens who complete suicide always act sad beforehand.

This is not true. A teen who completes suicide may appear irritable or withdrawn and also happy at times. Suicide can actually be a rather sudden response to a major stressful event.

MYTH: Teens who complete suicide spend a lot of time planning it.

This is not always true. Suicide may be planned, but it could also be an impulsive act. Whether it is planned or impulsive, suicide may feel like the best way to escape pain.

MYTH: Suicide among teens is rare.

This is false. Suicide is the second-leading cause of death among teenagers. Teens who struggle with mental health issues like depression as well as those who abuse drugs and alcohol are at a higher risk of taking their own life.

MYTH: Suicide is selfish.

That is an opinion — a judgment. But it's not what a suicidal person thinks. When someone is severely depressed, they think their family and the world would be better off without them. They feel as though they are a total failure and their life has no point or does not matter.

MYTH: Teens who complete suicide must have wanted suicide.

This is not true. Individuals who complete suicide want to end their pain. In almost all cases, they have tried to find other ways to end their pain but have been unsuccessful. For whatever reason, they feel that there is only one option left: dying.

MYTH: If you try to protect a suicidal person by taking away their method, they will just find another way to commit suicide.

This is not true. One study tracked 515 people who were saved before they jumped from the Golden Gate Bridge, and it found that, after decades, 90 percent were alive or had died from natural causes. Intervention can lead to help and save lives.

MYTH: People don't copycat.

This is not true. When someone completes suicide and it is reported in the news extensively, other people may "copycat" and complete suicide in the same way. Copycatting is a real problem, and dozens of studies have shown that pervasive coverage or reporting specific details can pave the way for copycats.

MYTH: Suicidal thoughts are rare.

This is not true. Suicidal thoughts run on a spectrum. *Fleeting* thoughts of suicide are fairly common. However, if these thoughts happen frequently, particularly when someone is struggling through a hard time, it could be a call for help.

What is less common is when someone makes a specific plan involving when, where, and how to kill themselves.

SUICIDE RISK FACTORS AND WARNING SIGNS

It's a sad truth: Some people are more at risk for suicide than others. Why? Some of these risk factors may be inherited, such as a family history of depression or suicide. Others, such as physical illnesses, may also contribute. And, of course, lifestyle choices may also increase the risk. Learn to recognize the risk factors for suicide, whether in your life or someone else's, and act to address them early, in whatever way you can. It may save a life.

Here is a list of suicide risk factors, according to the American Foundation for Suicide Prevention. Most of these have already been discussed in this book. Remember: Experiencing one or more of these doesn't mean someone *will* attempt suicide, but studies and statistics show that these conditions increase the risk that they might.

Suicide Risk Factors
- Previous suicide attempt(s)
- History of abuse, whether physical, psychological, or sexual
- Mental health conditions
- Serious physical illness or injury
- Traumatic brain injury
- Access to lethal means
- Prolonged stress

- Major traumatic life events (such as parental divorce, death of a loved one, romantic breakups, bullying)
- Exposure to the suicide of others

It's also worth remembering that just because someone *hasn't* experienced any of the risk factors named above doesn't mean they will *never* consider suicide. Even "popular" kids and good students attempt and sometimes complete suicide. Sometimes people are very good at hiding their problems, like depression, which doesn't discriminate. There is no single type of person who is always or never at risk.

As a result, learn and be on the lookout for the following warning signs, in yourself or in others. While suicide is sometimes an impulsive act, studies show that four out of five teen suicide attempts *are* preceded by clear warning signs. Even recognizing only one or two warning signs is cause for worry and action. Don't ignore, downplay, or dismiss any indication that someone may be thinking about suicide.

Teen Suicide Warning Signs

- Disinterest in favorite extracurricular activities
- Substance abuse
- Behavioral problems, such as reckless, aggressive, or self-destructive behavior
- Isolation, or withdrawing from family and friends
- Changes in sleep patterns: sleeping too much or too little

- Changes in eating habits: overeating, bingeing, or not eating
- Neglecting personal appearance: not showering or messy appearance
- Lack of concentration or extreme fatigue
- Declining grades
- Feeling depressed or hopeless
- Frequent complaints of boredom
- Talking about suicide in general or a preoccupation with death
- Searching for or considering methods
- Giving away personal possessions
- Saying goodbye

TAKE ACTION: HAVING A CONVERSATION AND GETTING HELP

Of course, the biggest, most obvious warning sign is when someone tells you that they are thinking about suicide or planning to kill themselves. Sometimes people say this directly. And sometimes they imply it very strongly by saying things like:

"I wish I were dead. Then I wouldn't have to deal with this."

"I want you to know the truth in case something happens to me."

"Don't worry. Soon I won't bother you anymore."

"If I only had some pills, I'd end things right now."

A person might fantasize about, or even draft, their suicide note, or they might behave very erratically, expressing bizarre or disturbing thoughts and swinging between extreme cheerfulness and extreme depression. These things are serious, urgent calls for help. They may indicate that someone already has a suicide plan, one they are ready to act on. Don't ignore these warning signs or hesitate if someone tells you they want to end their life.

Instead, do two things: talk to the person, and let an adult know.

Having a conversation about suicide is difficult. It's a hard topic to bring up. This is why many people hesitate even when someone is clearly troubled. So remember: People considering suicide want to end their pain. They often don't know how to deal with their feelings and problems, they see no other solutions, and they feel there is no one who cares or is willing to help. So simply by noticing and asking about someone's problems, you show the person that they are seen and that someone cares. Here are some examples of what you might say or how to start this conversation:

> "When you say, 'I don't want to be around anymore,' what do you mean? Tell me what's hurting."
>
> "I've noticed you've been avoiding me and all your friends. Why? I want to know what's going on. Will you talk to me about it?"
>
> "I'm really worried about you lately. If you tell me what's going on, maybe I can help."
>
> "Saying you want to die scares me. Thinking up a

suicide note isn't a joke. I care about you and want to know what's going on."

Regardless of the circumstances or how you start the conversation, the most important thing is to communicate your concern and understanding. Make sure your friend or loved one knows you're there to help and coming from a place of love. You don't have to solve their problems; in fact, you probably can't. As this book has discussed, truly healing someone's underlying problems can require professional medical or therapeutic help. But friends offer something just as important: a sympathetic ear and a loving heart. All people are helped when they can share their painful thoughts and feelings and be acknowledged.

In addition, let an adult you trust know. Tell them what's happening and what you fear. Don't try to handle this alone or keep it a secret with your friend. And if you have any reason to fear for someone's immediate safety, treat it like an emergency and take immediate action. Call their parents, your parents, and if necessary the police. For more advice about how to help someone, see chapter 15.

THE REALITY OF TEEN SUICIDE

As this book has hopefully made clear, teen suicide is a very real, very serious problem in the United States. If you doubt that, consider these eye-opening and even shocking national statistics:

- Girls attempt suicide twice as often as boys.
- Boys complete suicide four times more than girls.

- Teen suicide is on the rise. The number of suicides among adolescents aged ten to fourteen increased 70 percent from 2006 to 2016. From 2007 to 2015, the number of suicides among girls aged fifteen to nineteen doubled, while the rate for boys in the same age group increased 30 percent.
- While girls between the ages of ten and fourteen make up a small portion of total suicides, the rate in this group has experienced the largest percentage increase, tripling over a fifteen-year period, from 1999 to 2014.
- In 2015, 18 percent of high school students seriously considered suicide.
- About nine hundred thousand youths planned their suicides during episodes of major depression.
- Nearly 9 percent of high school students said they have tried killing themselves at least once.
- Stigma surrounding suicide can lead to under-reporting, so the actual number of suicides is most likely higher than estimates and statistics indicate.
- Suicide is the third-leading cause of death for people aged ten to twenty-four.
- More teenagers and young adults die from suicide than from cancer, heart disease, AIDS, birth defects, stroke, pneumonia, influenza, and chronic lung disease combined.
- Each day in the United States, there are, on average, more than 5,400 suicide attempts by young people in grades seven through twelve.

- Four out of five teens who attempt suicide give clear warning signs.
- Ninety percent of teens who kill themselves have some type of ongoing or recurring mental health problem, such as depression, anxiety, drug or alcohol abuse, PTSD, bipolar disorder, or a behavioral problem.
- In any given year, one youth completes suicide for every twenty-five who attempt it.

MY STORY

I know the impact of suicide and have firsthand knowledge of how suicide can unfold because my husband, Bill, completed suicide. He wasn't a teenager, but our story is a good example of many of the issues raised in this book: the toll of substance abuse and recurring mental health issues, how someone can hide problems and suicidal thoughts, and the warning signs that loved ones may notice without fully recognizing what they mean in time.

Who was Bill as a teenager? Picture a really perfect-looking football quarterback. The kind who would be on a movie poster — someone who made you want to watch the movie even if you didn't like football.

Then picture an amazing baseball pitcher.

Then picture a basketball player sculpted like an action figure.

Got that image in mind? That was Bill.

Bill grew up in Houston, Texas, and he excelled at all three of these sports. An outstanding athlete, Bill was voted "best dressed" in high school, and he was very popular with the girls because he was good-looking *and* nice. At six foot two and 150 pounds, he was pretty amazing in every way.

Then, when Bill was in college, one of his roommates introduced him to bodybuilding. Competitive bodybuilding is a dark sport because it requires steroid use to sculpt your body to look like a bodybuilder. Bill dropped out of college to continue this pursuit, training with Phil Pfister, also known as "Big Phil," who later went on to win the World's Strongest Man competition. At that time, Phil weighed more than four hundred pounds.

During this training, Bill added a hundred pounds of muscle, which was only possible because of steroids. Those became a regular part of Bill's life.

"They made me feel like Superman," he once told me. "I felt like I could do anything I set my mind to."

Yet along with these superhero-like feelings, Bill's personality changed. The sweet, friendly, athletic guy everyone loved disappeared. He became angry. After college, he had married, but he began lying to his wife about where he was going and what he was doing, and soon they divorced. Bill stopped calling his parents to check in with them. He spent at least four hours of every day at the gym, utterly obsessed with his physique. And in his spare time, he slept.

Another lesson from Bill's experience is that steroid use is very, very dangerous. Today, more than 1.5 million teens admit to using steroids, and the median age for steroid use is fifteen. An NCAA survey found that 50 percent of college athletes started steroid use in high school, where it's very common. Girls are actually the largest growing steroid-using population, with one in twenty using.

Even nonathletes use steroids to enhance their personal appearance. These people are called "mirror athletes."

For seven years, Bill consumed GHB (gamma hydroxy-butyrate), a growth-hormone steroid, daily. Taking small amounts of this substance was supposed to help increase muscle mass, and apparently everyone in the bodybuilding world used GHB, trying to get that small edge over the competition. At the time, GHB could be purchased at your local nutrition store.

Today, GHB is referred to as the date-rape drug and is an illegal substance. Unfortunately, because it can be made at home, this drug has made a comeback in recent years. It's known to cause euphoria in small amounts, but when mixed with alcohol, it can lead to sedation, coma, and even death. GHB is no joke.

Then, Bill decided to pursue a job opportunity in California and start a new life. In California, he could no longer purchase GHB, so his body went through the detox process cold turkey. For weeks, Bill suffered nausea, vomiting, cold sweats, and insomnia. To battle the insomnia and anxiety, he began taking sleeping pills and sedatives.

However, Bill's new career as a personal trainer took off. He acquired enough clients to open up his own gym. Not long thereafter, a mutual friend introduced the two of us.

Life is not like the movies, but our first dates definitely felt like one. I finally understood the expression "I feel like I'm on cloud nine." When you really hit it off with someone and feel like they get you and you get them, *and* you can still be yourself, well, it's an incredible feeling. That's what it was like when Bill and I met, and after two years, in July 2005, we got married. Our wedding day was one of the happiest of my life.

Three years later, the effects of Bill's past began to affect his — and our — present.

First, two people we knew completed suicide. One was a trainer at the gym, Dave. He rode his motorcycle to a secluded area and shot himself. Then there was a member of our gym, Alex. He set himself on fire and jumped off the bluff near our home just two days after he had been in our gym, talking to us about his dreams and struggles.

"What could possibly be so bad in their lives that they would choose to die?" Bill asked me. I had only an inkling then of what I know now: They probably struggled with a lot, and they were good at hiding it. Plus, we didn't know how to read the warning signs.

In 2008, Bill and I decided to make a major life change. The US economy had taken a big nosedive, which created hard times for many people. We decided to sell our gym and move to a Mexican town called Rosarito, just south of the California border. We had spent many weekends there and enjoyed it.

The first three months were awesome — almost like being on a luxurious vacation. We worked out, took Spanish classes, explored the sights, and dined out. But once summer was over and the tourists went home, the novelty wore off and Bill's insomnia worsened. Bill's identity was wrapped up in being a successful gym owner, and he wasn't one anymore. He missed, and needed, the daily validation that his physique was a source of admiration, which is what a gym full of customers provided.

Day after day, he paced our condo, screaming, "Get me out of this box! I hate it here!"

Very quickly, this man I loved so deeply became a virtual stranger to me. He seemed, in fact, unaware of my presence. I knew he was sick and needed help. All of the meds he took did nothing to soothe him. Because of that, he stopped using prescription medication for his insomnia, thinking he'd feel better taking fewer medications, and the withdrawal was a big reason he was acting out of his mind.

We moved back to California, and I searched desperately for a psychiatrist who could help him, but they only changed medications when one wasn't working for his anxiety and sleeplessness. Soon he was taking more than fifteen different prescriptions. The layering of all the different medications only made Bill more paranoid and more depressed. Counseling didn't work, since Bill was in denial. I didn't know it then, but Bill needed hospitalization and to enter a detox program.

Bill said he felt hopeless and worthless. "You would be so much better off without me," he would tell me. "Why do you stay with me? All I do is drag you down. I'm just a burden to you."

I called Bill's father to tell him what was happening. He broke down in tears, his voice faltering. "Bill has two grandmothers who were hospitalized for depression and...a suicide attempt."

Thus, on top of being overmedicated, Bill was at risk for inheriting depression. Further, as a child, Bill had felt abandoned by his parents, who traveled extensively. This fed his paranoia that I might leave him, but at the time, I didn't realize the significance of these risk factors.

In addition, Bill struggled to go to work, though he had only a few training clients left. He would come home and crawl into bed. We never did anything social and rarely left the house. As with the others, I didn't recognize his isolation and withdrawal as suicide warning signs, since I was completely focused on getting him treatment. I believed it was just a matter of time before he got better and returned to his old self.

One morning I woke up to find a note Bill had left for me.

Baby,
You need to move on with your life and find somebody better. I can't do this anymore.
Love, Bill

I could hear him in the shower, so I ran to the bathroom, screaming at the top of my lungs, "What is this?"

Bill confessed that the previous night he had taken an entire bottle of sedatives, but it didn't work and he had woken up.

I wasn't sure whether to believe him. How could consuming an entire bottle of pills do nothing? I suspected, as many loved ones do, that this was just a cry for attention, not a genuine suicide attempt. However, I persuaded Bill to admit himself to Mission Hospital in Laguna Beach, where they put him on a three-day involuntary suicide watch. Afterward, Bill was released without further treatment.

A few weeks later, Bill left the house early in the morning, didn't say where he was going, and left his phone on the kitchen counter. By early evening, when there was still no sign of him, I became panicked, called the police, and filed a missing persons report. A few minutes after the police arrived at our apartment to take my statement and start their search, Bill walked through the front door. He was completely unaware of the chaos he'd created.

"Where have you been?" I asked.

"Down at the train tracks pacing for the last eight hours," he said. I realized that the top of his head was blistered, and he hadn't even noticed. "I needed to get away and have some time to think."

I foolishly accepted Bill at his word. Only afterward did I realize that Bill hadn't been thinking. He'd been planning and rehearsing his death.

Four weeks later, Bill took a turn for the worse. His paranoia skyrocketed — about everything — but particularly about his belief that I was having a secret affair. One night, he trapped me in the bathroom by blockading the door with his outstretched arms.

"What's your secret boyfriend's name?" he demanded.

"Stop being ridiculous!" I said. "Let me out." He refused to budge, staring me down. "Bill, you're scaring me!" I yelled.

I fought my way past him and grabbed my purse. I said, "I love you, but right now I'm afraid of you. I'm going to spend the night at my sister's." I thought spending a night apart would help him realize how ridiculous he was acting and then everything would return to normal.

How wrong I was.

The next morning, I drove home to change clothes and

go to work. Bill was gone, and on the phone, I noticed multiple missed calls from Bill's parents.

I dialed Texas, where they lived, and Bill's mother answered.

I figured they must have heard about our fight the night before, but before I could reassure her not to worry, Bill's mother cut me off in a flat, detached voice: "Kristi," she said, "Bill's been in an accident. He's been hit by a train. I think he might be dead."

She told me that Bill's father was actually in town, staying at a local hotel. He'd arrived late the previous night, having flown from Houston to San Diego, and then taken a train from San Diego to our town. He had become very worried about Bill, who had called him the previous morning to say that he was in trouble and his brain was scrambled.

On the train, Bill's father had had to sit through a four-hour delay when there was an accident just outside our station. Apparently, a man had stepped onto the train tracks, spread his arms out to his side like Jesus on the cross, and stared into the eyes of the train engineer. At such short notice, the engineer was powerless to stop the train in time, and a thousand tons of steel struck my husband head on.

It wasn't until the next morning that Bill's father realized it had been his son standing in front of that train.

Chapter 13

FINDING HOPE
IN THE DARKNESS

My husband didn't believe in hope. After his suicide, I don't think I did, either. Now that time has passed and I've gained more knowledge and a whole lot of perspective, I wish I could go back and make Bill see the hope that is all around — the hope that is attainable.

Because there *is* hope.

Does that statement sound trite? Maybe. But let's back up. What *is* hope?

Hope is an optimistic attitude based on expectations of positive outcomes in one's life or the world at large.

A person who has a high level of hope has healthier habits, sleeps better, exercises more, eats healthier, gets sick less often, and is more likely to have less depression and to survive a life-threatening illness.

Students who have hope usually have higher grades. Hope, in fact, is a bigger predictor than SAT scores of who will finish college.

Hope sounds pretty great, right? Aside from all these physical and mental benefits, *hope can save your life.*

There is no better example of this than Gavin, whom you met in the introduction. Here's the rest of his story:

GAVIN'S STORY, CONTINUED

I already told you about the darkest moment of my life — as I stood at the top of a parking structure thinking how easy it would be to jump and be free of the pain I felt every day. I was already sleeping as much as I could every day. Wasn't the next step to sleep…forever?

It's funny — or miraculous, really — that I chose that particular parking structure. As I stood at the top contemplating my death, I had the perfect view of Mission Hospital. I saw the large sign with the familiar cross logo I'd seen countless times. But this time, it seemed to call to me, telling me to come inside and get help.

Knowing what my alternative was, I listened. Before I could rethink my decision, I drove to the hospital and asked for help. I went into detox for five days to get the drugs out of my system. Detoxing felt like I was dying, but after the moment I had on the parking structure, I still knew I was safer within the walls of the hospital than outside.

Once clean, I had to face my life without the help of drugs. But I wasn't alone. I spent the next six months in treatment for substance abuse and depression, then I continued therapy for one year.

Do you know what happened?

I began to realize that my life matters.

See, I didn't know what depression looked like. I just thought something was wrong with me. My brain was crying for help and I didn't know it. Once I got that help, life improved. A lot. Had I been taught the warning signs of depression, my high school experience may have been different. It might have been a lot happier and a lot less scary.

I still have depression. It's a mental illness that isn't going to just disappear. But now I have the coping skills to deal with it. When I feel down, I *know* tomorrow will be a better day. I make sure I'm doing what I love and that I'm surrounded by family and friends who love me, too.

Maybe you hurt like I did, or maybe you know someone who sounds like who I used to be. If you do, I promise, there is hope.

There is hope I didn't know existed during my darkest of times. But now I know: Depression is a disease that can be treated.

Whether it's you or a friend, there is treatment and hope. Things can turn around.

This book has all the tactics, steps, and resources I used to recover and find hope, and I promise they can help you or a friend who needs it.

DEVELOPING HOPE

I know Gavin personally, and you know what? He is one of the most hopeful people I know. He's a great example of how people who are hopeful don't just have a goal, they have a strategy to achieve that goal and the motivation to carry it out. Hope is the belief that the future will be better than the present and that the power to make it better resides within you.

People often lose hope when they focus on obstacles instead of goals or on what excites and inspires them. Just thinking of happy things can remind us of what hope feels like. Doing what we enjoy can boost our confidence and mood, and spending time with hopeful people is also beneficial because — guess what? — hope is contagious.

Even when you feel completely hopeless, the great news is that it's possible to develop hope. All it takes is reminding yourself of what's good in your life. Right now, try this simple exercise. Write a list of all the people, things, and activities that make you feel happy, loved, comforted, motivated, and inspired. They don't all need to be profound. Here are a few examples to get you started:

- Friends and family who love and believe in you
- Favorite activities, sports, and hobbies (whether you're good at them or not)
- Times in your life when you felt whole, happy, and loved
- Favorite locations that are beautiful and relaxing (like the beach or your childhood backyard)
- Acts of kindness someone has done for you
- Acts of kindness you have performed for others
- Favorite songs, poems, and books
- Personal achievements or accomplishments you feel proud of (whether you won an award or not)
- Things you hope to achieve or do in the future

Now put this list somewhere you'll see it every day. Why? Because it can be easy to forget all the things that make life worth living, especially when we're struggling with difficulties and depression, so we develop hope in dark times by reminding ourselves to stay focused on what's good.

DEPRESSION IS A THIEF AND A LIAR

The other reason to keep this list handy is because depression is a thief and a liar. It's a thief because it robs you of hope — hope that you'll feel better, hope that the darkness will lift, hope that the emptiness will fill up and you'll feel motivated and excited again, hope that you'll actually get through it.

Depression is a liar because it makes you feel like it will last forever. That is the nature of the disorder, and it's important to remind yourself that depression is not a permanent state. It's temporary, and it can be treated and overcome.

Depression has a way of distorting our outlook so that we only notice the bleakest parts of the world. The darkness distorts reality until we believe this distortion *is* reality. We may even start to think that we have always been depressed, as if nothing else has ever existed, and even our precious memories of joy and happiness feel distant or unreal.

Of course, no one wants to feel this way, which is why many people don't want to admit they are depressed. Doing so would require admitting the very real and painful experiences that sparked the feelings of hopelessness. However, admitting "I feel hopeless and depressed" can actually be a positive first step. That doesn't mean you believe life is hopeless; rather, it's honestly recognizing and admitting how you *feel*. Identifying a problem is necessary to fix it, and so the next question to ask is why. If negative emotions are suffocating joy and robbing you of hope, see if you can identify possible solutions to feel better. For instance, many people with depression feel alone. They feel no one understands what they're going through and that they have no one to talk to.

If that's true for you, then a good action to take would be to find someone to talk to, someone who understands, so you don't feel alone. What do you do when hope feels unfamiliar or impossible? It is important to use a wide variety of coping strategies to help overcome depression. Keeping a list of good things and happy memories can help, and what follows are more techniques.

COPING STRATEGIES FOR DEPRESSION

To cope with depression, or any mental health issue, you need a support system. This includes therapists and doctors who handle any treatment as well as caring friends and family who provide love and understanding. Don't be afraid to request emotional support: Ask others to help you remember the good times when you feel down and to share your joy whenever you experience it. Then make a deal to do the same for them, since helping others is a great way to forget our own troubles.

Every day, participate in activities that you love. Do something that brings you pleasure, even if you don't feel like doing it. Listen to a song you love, watch a favorite old movie, or play a sport that makes you feel good. Take a walk in nature. For me, sitting down with an inspirational book is a lifeline. It helps me tap into a private, personal world — even if it's just for a few minutes.

Pleasurable activities raise dopamine levels in the brain, causing us to feel better — not to mention these activities are a welcome distraction from depression. They provide glimmers of hope that we *can* feel whole and healthy again. This is why the list of life's good things and a support team of caring people are so important. They help us see through the big lie of depression and remember that no matter how hopeless we feel in any particular moment, that feeling won't last. Hope and happiness will return, and we will feel much better in the future.

That said, don't worry or feel overwhelmed if coping with depression is harder or takes longer than you wish. Don't increase your frustration by expecting too much too quickly. Another good coping strategy is to make a list every morning of small goals, and then strive to check off as many as you can by bedtime. This can include obligations like going to a therapy appointment and chores like washing the dishes. But focus on easy activities that foster joy and hope, things like "call a friend, take a walk, write in a journal, doodle for ten minutes, compliment a coworker." Do things that avoid isolation and help create a more positive outlook.

Finally, I suggest creating a meditation for hope that you repeat daily, or several times a day. This can be as simple as repeating an inspiring quote to yourself whenever you feel doubt creep in or listening to soothing background music while you meditate. Here are a few good quotes to consider:

- What you think or wish, do.
- Be your own person because no one can take that away from you.
- Why stop dreaming when you wake up? Expect only the best from life, and take action to get it.
- No matter the number of times you fail, keep trying to succeed.

- Don't lose hope or faith. Faith and hope work hand in hand.
- To be without hope is like being without goals; what are you working toward?

See chapter 14 for more suggestions on how to create a healthy lifestyle and cope with depression. In order to change, we must act on our hope every day until we accomplish what we want. With good treatment, effective coping strategies, and compassionate support, we can feel better. Our heaviness will get lighter, and our world will become brighter.

Remember, no matter how hopeless you feel, hope and relief are around the corner. They are real, and they are possible.

Commit to yourself and your dreams, and take action. Discover, or rediscover, the amazing person you are — which is the same person you've always been!

Chapter 14

CREATING A HEALTHY LIFESTYLE

In the classic comic strip *Li'l Abner*, the character Joe Btfsplk constantly has a dark rain cloud following him wherever he goes. Do you ever feel like that? The rest of the world seems sunny and fine, but that character can't escape the nonstop pouring rain.

That's what depression and other mental illnesses are like: all-consuming. But unlike the cartoon, there's nothing funny about it.

However, as I say throughout, even the most severe mental issues are treatable. Therapy and medication are one type of treatment, and what's best depends on each person, their issues, and the advice of doctors. Another form of treatment is to create a healthier lifestyle. The last chapter discussed coping strategies for dealing with depression whenever it arises. Lifestyle changes are different: They adjust the way you live every day in order to keep depression at bay and reclaim your life.

Depression and anxiety are diseases, and like most diseases, your lifestyle can affect them. Both your body and your brain require proper care and fuel, which is what a healthy lifestyle provides. Think about it: If you had heart disease, would you eat hamburgers and fries and expect to get better? No. To get better, you'd eat better, exercise more, and so on. It's no different with mental illness. Good lifestyle habits can help your brain function optimally. They won't "cure" depression, but they help you cope with its symptoms and minimize the impact and duration of depressed episodes. Like an athlete, the right lifestyle makes you emotionally stronger and more resilient.

Unfortunately, depression has two best buds: apathy and lack of energy. These make it hard to do anything. If this describes you, be patient with yourself. Celebrate each accomplishment, and don't give yourself a hard time when you slip up. Take small steps, and remember that each step counts. If you take a few positive steps each day, you will find yourself making progress and feeling better — slowly but surely.

DEPRESSION REQUIRES PROFESSIONAL TREATMENT

The lifestyle strategies in this chapter are tools to help you cope with any psychological or emotional issues and to empower you to live a healthier life. That said, if you or someone you know has depression or any other mental health issue, these tools are only a supplement to professional treatment — *not* a replacement. A "healthy lifestyle" includes all the things you do to help yourself feel and live better. But you can't overcome depression all by yourself. And if there's one message I hope you take from this book, it's that it's okay to ask for help. That begins with talking to and getting help from those closest to you: your parents, teachers, friends, and so on. But this also often includes getting help from doctors and therapists. These trained professionals are armed with the knowledge and resources to identify what's going on in your situation and to develop an appropriate, effective treatment plan. If you haven't already sought medical advice, and you believe you're struggling with a mental health issue, please do so.

That said, the ultimate success of any treatment plan depends on the individual, who must embrace the plan and make the necessary lifestyle changes to support it. In other words, healing is always a joint effort. No one can heal themselves alone, but others can't heal someone without that person's cooperation and determination. Whatever your situation, and whatever your treatment plan and the people involved, just know that everyone has the same goal: to help you feel healthier, happier, and more positive so that you can live a healthier, happier life, both now and in future.

TIPS FOR A HEALTHY LIFESTYLE

Move Every Day

When you're depressed, just climbing out of bed can seem utterly impossible, let alone working out. But exercise is a powerful fighter of depression and anxiety and one of the most important tools for relieving symptoms. Exercise increases your body temperature, which helps produce a feeling of warmth and releases endorphins, the feel-good chemicals in your brain that help improve mood. Exercise also helps prevent relapse once you're well. Any type of movement can make a difference; find something you enjoy so you'll stick with it. It can be skateboarding, walking the dog, or dancing to a favorite song. Even a ten-minute walk can improve your mood. Work your way up to sixty minutes of exercise per day (in total, not all at once). Ask a friend or family member to join you; exercising with another person provides support and encouragement.

Eat Well

Here's an interesting fact: 95 percent of the body's serotonin (the neurotransmitter responsible for regulating sleep, appetite, and mood) is produced in the gastrointestinal tract. This says a lot about the link between your brain and your gut. People with low serotonin levels are much more likely to suffer from depression, anxiety, and insomnia, as well as exhibit poor impulse control and experience thoughts of suicide. If your gastrointestinal tract isn't functioning as it should, it's possible you're not producing the serotonin you need for a balanced, healthy brain.

You probably already know that what you eat can have a great effect on how you feel. In fact, studies have shown that people whose diets revolve around whole, unprocessed food — like a Mediterranean diet, which is rich in vegetables and seafood and low in grains and dairy — have a reduced risk of depression and other mental illnesses compared to those who eat a diet containing processed foods and sugars. So don't jeopardize your mental health because of your diet. Limit the amount of "junk" you put in your body, such as packaged snacks, sugar, energy and soft drinks, and fast food. Instead, eat more fresh fruits, vegetables, lean meats, and seafood. Pay attention to see how different foods make you feel. If you feel better without it, don't eat it!

Socialize

Feeling isolated from family and friends, and from other humans in general, can have a catastrophic effect on your psychological health. This is why isolation is used as a form of punishment in prison and even a form of torture for prisoners of war. The thing about depression is that its symptoms are cyclical: When you're depressed, you don't want to be around people, but isolating yourself just exacerbates depression. When this happens to you, practice having faith; trust that connecting with others will help you feel better. This isn't just anecdotal; it's scientifically proven.

Here's the catch. Social media is no substitute for face-to-face interactions, which are best for reducing feelings of depression. A supportive text or a message from a friend can certainly lift your spirits, but meeting someone in person is best. So accept (or offer) an invitation, attend the school dance, and stay up to talk to your siblings or parents. And if you can't meet someone, call and talk to them. It certainly won't hurt, and the evidence suggests it'll actually help you feel better.

Get Sunlight

I know, I know, spending too much time in the sun increases the risk for skin cancer. Then again, too little sun hurts our mental well-being. The body is an incredible system that regulates itself using hormones and neurotransmitters. Above, I mention how adequate serotonin levels are critical for our mood (and much more). As it turns out, our bodies are programmed to produce serotonin in the sunlight, and they produce melatonin — the hormone that helps us feel sleepy — in the darkness. So whenever you feel listless, tired, or unmotivated, getting out in the sun can help. In fact, people with seasonal affective disorder — depression caused by lack of sunlight during the winter months — are often treated with light therapy to help them produce the serotonin their body needs to feel better. In a way, we're like plants — without sunlight, we become listless and wither away.

Make getting outside part of your routine. Put on sunscreen and take a walk around the block, read a book on your porch, or eat your lunch on a park bench. Nature is healing, so enjoy it whenever you can.

Focus on Others

Here's an interesting paradox: When we focus entirely on our own needs, this often makes us feel *worse,* but focusing on someone else's needs makes us feel better. Helping another person can give you a major mood boost. Like exercise and sunlight, it doesn't have to be extreme — perhaps giving a friend a ride home from school or contributing to a canned food drive. Studies have shown that people who have compassionate goals (goals to positively influence another's life) show fewer symptoms of depression, have less conflict in relationships, and feel better about themselves.

Volunteer, lend an ear to a friend, go to a friend's concert or game, or shovel an elderly neighbor's sidewalk.

Vent When Necessary

Holding in pent-up feelings and emotions isn't healthy, so when you feel like you're going to burst, do so in a safe way. Sometimes that might mean screaming into a pillow, but more often, the best ways to vent are to write your thoughts and feelings down in a journal or talk to a sympathetic, caring friend, family member, or therapist. If you want, ask the person to just listen, without commenting or giving advice, and then describe what you're feeling (start with "I feel"). Naming emotions can help you identify negative feelings and depression, which is an important step in treatment. Once you've vented, if you feel safe, give the other person a chance to talk. You never know — they may have some valuable insight that can comfort you or change your perspective.

Get Enough Sleep

There really aren't exceptions to this rule: Everything seems worse when you're sleep deprived. That rule can certainly be applied to depression and anxiety. Sleep is another one of those cyclical symptoms of depression: You're depressed and you can't sleep, but lack of sleep only makes depression worse, and on it goes. Sleep is critical because it's a restorative state; it allows the body to heal and rejuvenate. Fatigue from lack of sleep can also make it harder to get the physical activity the body needs to function properly.

How much sleep should teens be getting? The ideal

amount of sleep for teens is nine to ten hours each night. If you're not getting enough sleep, start now. If you have a hard time falling asleep, limit your caffeine intake and turn off electronics at least an hour before getting in bed. Be consistent with your bedtime, even on the weekends. If insomnia is persistent, talk to your doctor as soon as possible. Getting enough sleep helps you be more optimistic and empowers you to make better decisions.

Avoid Drugs and Alcohol

When someone suffers from depression or another mental health issue, it's all too easy to use drugs and alcohol as a coping mechanism. As I discuss in chapter 10, this creates a vicious cycle that can lead to abuse, dependence, and addiction. Substance abuse is particularly dangerous for teens because their brains are still developing. Drugs and alcohol can interfere with that development and even permanently alter the way the brain works.

Think of it this way: Depression is a chemical imbalance in the brain. Alcohol and drugs alter the chemistry in the brain. Together, they form a one-two punch that robs you of your most valuable asset — your true self. If you feel the urge to self-medicate, talk to a doctor or a therapist and develop healthy coping mechanisms that help you feel better while protecting your (amazing) developing brain.

Do Something Fun

Depression could also be called "fun deficiency." It's really, really hard to feel down and depressed when you're having fun. In fact, countless studies have shown that doing something you love can dramatically reduce symptoms of depression. That's because "fun" triggers the production of dopamine, which controls the pleasure center in the brain. It doesn't matter what you consider fun — it might be bungee jumping, fishing, or playing games with friends — just do it. Many mental illnesses (especially depression) undermine the motivation to do anything. So even if you have to force yourself, do something every day that you love. Chances are, once you're *doing* that activity, you'll actually have...*fun*, and as I say, it's really hard to feel depressed when you're having fun.

Relax to Recharge

Relaxation is a state in which your body can recharge and rejuvenate, relieving stress and boosting feelings of joy and well-being. Relaxation is different than lethargy, listlessness, and oversleeping, which are common symptoms of depression. Relaxation isn't about doing nothing. It's about actively calming the emotions and clearing the mind to lessen anxiety, improve thinking, and increase energy. Meditation is one of the most common and effective ways to practice relaxation, but yoga is another ideal activity, since it's all about meditative, gentle physical exercise. If you can, join a yoga or meditation class; these are both great ways to learn and great ways to incorporate regular relaxation into your life. Some yoga studios offer donation-based classes, or to practice at home, you can find books, online yoga videos, and various meditation apps.

However, these aren't for everyone, and you can practice whatever relaxation techniques that work for you. Try two minutes of deep breathing in the morning, a walk in the woods, or watching the sunset on a park bench. Be creative and curious and explore the best ways to relax and recharge your body and mind.

Challenge Negative Thoughts

Depression in particular puts a negative spin on everything, especially the way you see yourself and how you see the future. That's the lie of depression: the feeling that bad things will continue to happen for the rest of your life and there's nothing you can do about it. These thoughts can become overwhelming, playing on a constant loop. Indeed, these negative thoughts might reflect a lifelong pattern of thinking that's so automatic you're not even aware of it. When negative thoughts arise, try challenging them. Stand up to the voice of depression and ask, "Is this thought true?" Step back and consider the thought like an objective observer: "Is there another way of looking at the situation or another explanation? Would the situation look the same if I didn't have depression or anxiety?" Most of all, ask yourself: "If a good friend had this thought, what would I tell them and how would I help them?" Listen to this other, more compassionate voice. You may surprise yourself as you develop a more balanced perspective.

Develop Healthy Routines

Everyone develops routines and habits. These are the things we do almost automatically every day, in the same way, at the same times — mostly because we did the same things yesterday, and the day before, and so on. Habits are habits because they reinforce themselves. Research varies regarding how long — in days or repetitions — it takes to form a habit, but once formed, they are increasingly harder to break the longer they continue.

So create healthy habits based on the lifestyle tips in this chapter. For now, don't worry about changing bad habits; just focus on creating new, healthier routines. Designate specific times each day to exercise, relax, and have fun. Make a habit of calling friends and family members — or better yet, see them in person. Establish a healthy sleep routine, with a firm bedtime and wake-up time, then stick to it every day. Set regular times for study or to do homework. And be sure to make a routine for activities you enjoy, whether listening to music, watching TV, or being creative. It's easier to develop good habits when we look forward to the activity.

Prepare in advance for the coming week. Be organized. Note any schedule changes, special appointments, or other obligations, and tailor your routine around those. Your body and your brain will function better when they know what to expect.

Developing new habits certainly doesn't happen overnight. You may have already tried to develop a better habit and learned how hard it can be. There's a reason gyms are filled to capacity in January, after everyone makes New Year's resolutions to lose weight and get in shape, but look like ghost towns in March or April, when motivation wanes. However, get this: Teens have a distinct advantage over adults when it comes to creating healthy routines. Their brains are still developing rapidly, and they are more adaptable. Plus, the routines and habits you create now are more likely to stick with you for the rest of your life.

Make them good ones.

THE FUTURE IS BRIGHT

Throughout my career, I've had the honor of working with, talking to, and teaching teens. I am constantly in awe of their ambition, creativity, positivity, passion, and kindness. My hope for all the teen readers of this book is that, as you continually learn, grow, and evolve, you find ways to harness these characteristics for your own benefit and the benefit of others. If you currently have or are dealing with a mental health issue, it may be difficult to recognize all the ways your talents and abilities can enrich your life and the lives of those around you. That's why it's so important to be able to recognize and identify these issues in yourself or in a friend or family member. What looks perfect on paper rarely is. Everyone — you, me, everyone — has challenges, disappointments, illnesses, and traumas they deal with every day. When you recognize and address whatever is lurking *beneath the surface,* it loses power over you, allowing you to become the person you were always meant to be: simply incredible.

Chapter 15

REACHING OUT:
HELPING A FRIEND

If you recognize — perhaps after reading the symptoms and warning signs of a particular mental health issue in this book — that someone you love might be drowning beneath the surface, the question becomes: How can you help? Of course, every situation is different, so evaluate the best approach for yourself. However, the essence of helping others is simple: Reach out and listen, be compassionate, and get assistance as necessary.

REACH OUT AND LISTEN

If a friend or loved one seems depressed, or has shown warning signs of suicidal thoughts, the first and most important thing is to start a conversation and ask them what's going on. Don't assume you know what the problem is. Instead, ask them to share what's happening beneath the surface. In whatever way is appropriate for your relationship, do the following:

- Let them know you care.
- Ask if they're having problems and what they are.
- Listen to what they say.
- Offer sympathy, reassurance, and kindness.
- Tell them you are on their side.
- Ask them how you can help.

If someone doesn't want to talk about their problems, respect their privacy, but continue to reach out in friendly ways. In fact, text messages and social media can actually be a great tool for staying connected to someone who resists sharing or who isn't around to talk with in person. Sometimes, a little note of love and understanding sent in a simple text can go a long way.

Other strategies for reaching out include inviting the person to join you in daily activities or asking if you can join them in something they do. Then simply be supportive, and with your presence let them know that you care and they are not alone.

EXPRESS COMPASSION AND UNDERSTANDING

When someone shares their problems and struggles with you, the most important response is compassion and understanding. You don't need to solve their problems or have all the answers. You might even know what to say. That's okay. Sometimes it's hard to put feelings and thoughts into words. Here are some examples of the kinds of caring comments that can help someone going through a rough time. Feel free to rephrase these in your own way:

I'm always here for you, even when times are bad. I
     love you for who you are.

I'm on your side. We're a team.

You are important to me.

I can't imagine how hard this is for you, but I want to
     help in any way I can.

You are not alone.

You are a sensitive person and care so much for
     others.

This is an illness, and it's nothing to be ashamed of.
     It can happen to anyone.

I understand that you want to solve this by yourself,
     but if you let me help, we'll make it together.

I'm a good listener, so pour out your feelings. Is there
     anything I can do?

You make my life better just by being in it. I will
     always have your back.

Don't let darkness steal the beautiful person inside.
     You are never a burden.

I'm not going anywhere.

I'm beginning to understand how loud silence can
     be. Forgive me for not standing still enough to
     hear yours. I'm listening.

When communicating with texts, it's common to add
positive emojis or emoticons to convey emotion or to reinforce your words. But don't rely on pictures to get your
point across. *Be sure to also actually say or write what you
mean.*

Resist Judgment, Anger, and Frustration

It's not easy to talk to someone about depression, addiction, suicide, and other issues. Just the fact that someone is willing to talk is huge. It means they feel safe enough to share things that might be embarrassing or shameful, such as mistakes they've made and bad things they've done (to themselves or others). In this situation, it can be natural to feel frustrated or even angry at someone — perhaps even for not sharing their problems sooner. Someone's problems might feel overwhelming and scary, or you might think the person is overreacting. Or you may feel that, despite claiming otherwise, someone isn't being completely honest, that they are hiding or lying and refusing to admit the whole truth.

If this happens, resist the urge to judge someone or dismiss their feelings. Try not to express anger or frustration. Indeed, some reactions *sound* like they are trying to be helpful, but they are really ways to push someone away or invalidate their issues or feelings. Be aware if you make any comments like the following, and try to avoid them:

> Take your mind off of it and just go and have fun.
> There are a lot of people who have it worse than you do. Stop your pity party.
> Just get out and do something. It's all in your head.
> You'll be fine after a good night's sleep.
> Stop playing the victim and grow up already. You'll get over it.
> You have no reason to be unhappy. Things really aren't that bad.
> You don't look depressed.

You're doing this to attract attention. I've had to deal
with tougher things.

No one ever said life was fair. You're bringing this on
yourself. You're always so negative.

GET HELP

Reaching out and talking to someone who's struggling or
having suicidal thoughts might literally be a lifesaving conversation. But what about tomorrow? And the next day? As I
advise throughout this book, if you know or suspect someone is at risk for suicide and needs help, *tell someone*. Get
help. Now is not the time to keep secrets; your friend's life is
far too valuable.

However, while I always encourage teens to talk to someone if they or a friend is at risk, I also understand that this
"simple" piece of advice can be extremely complicated, depending on the situation. For example, a friend might con-
fide in you and ask you to promise not to tell anyone or not
to tell certain people. They trust you to keep their secrets,
and if you tell others, it may feel like a betrayal.

Every situation and friendship is unique, so there isn't
one right answer to this problem. I frequently advise teens to
ask themselves whether breaking a friend's trust will get the
person the genuine help they need. If the answer is a clear
yes, then do what's necessary to get that help. One situation
when you should never hesitate to reach out is if someone
threatens suicide and you fear they may be in immediate
danger. In that situation, you should always call 911.

In situations where there is no immediate risk of harm,
consider the pros and cons of all the people you might

approach and choose the best ones. The friend's parents are sometimes the best, most obvious choice — unless the friend has a troubled relationship with them, and you think telling your friend's parents could exacerbate problems. Most of the time, speaking with *your* parents, or a trusted relative, can be a good first choice. They might help you get clarity and guidance on what to do for your friend, and just as importantly, they can give you the support you need, since helping a friend in trouble can be confusing, difficult, scary, and painful.

You also probably know other adults whom you trust. This could be a teacher, counselor, clergy member, coach, or family friend. It might feel safest to talk to someone who doesn't know your friend, someone outside the situation, who might have a more objective perspective and can help guide you to find resources, and so on.

Helping a friend in crisis can be really tough. They may feel alone, and you may feel alone trying to help them. Neither of you may feel safe talking to or trusting *any* adult you know. In that situation, call one of the national helplines listed in the resources. Text them and visit their websites. These are free and confidential, and they are staffed by qualified professionals whose job is to help people in crisis, especially when they feel they have nowhere else to turn. These professionals are trained to intervene when callers threaten to harm themselves or others (by contacting the appropriate emergency response personnel), but their main goal is to listen and provide people with the guidance they need.

The bottom line is that there is *always* someone you can reach out to for help, even when it feels like there isn't.

ACKNOWLEDGMENTS

Writing this book was more rewarding than I ever could have imagined, as it empowered me to deliver a message of hope and help to those struggling most. As I continue every day to process the grief of losing my husband to suicide, I am buoyed up by the purpose I've found in the wake of that tragedy.

To Bill: Thank you from the bottom of my heart for the good memories — those that constantly motivate me to help those who are struggling as you were.

This book never would have been possible without Sheila Peterson, who believed in my mission and whose shared passion for mental health awareness and suicide prevention made this book a reality.

I'm eternally grateful to Kristen Price and Juliet Ekinaka for their hard work and dedication. I couldn't ask for a better team.

To my mom, Val; my sisters, Deb, Viki, and Jen; and my

brother, Todd: Thanks for all your support and encouragement.

To my agent, Paul Levine: Thank you for believing in me and in this book. Your dedication opened life-changing doors.

To the publishing team at New World Library: Georgia Hughes, editorial director; Kim Corbin, senior publicist; Kristen Cashman, managing editor; Tracy Cunningham, art director; and Tona Pearce Myers, production director; as well as Jeff Campbell, editor extraordinaire: Thank you for believing in my mission, and for helping me get this important book into the hands of those who need it most — our nation's teens.

To the teens reading this book: Thank you for the honesty, vulnerability, and faith you've shown simply by opening it. Please know that, along with everyone else who loves you, I'm in your corner and wishing you the best.

ENDNOTES

p. 4   *Unfortunately, nearly forty-five thousand Americans die by suicide each year*: "Suicide and Self-Inflicted Injuries," National Center for Health Statistics, Centers for Disease Control and Prevention, last updated March 17, 2017, https://www.cdc.gov/nchs /fastats/suicide.htm.

p. 13   *In fact, fifteen* million *kids in the United States have parents with depression*: National Research Council and Institute of Medicine Committee on Depression, Parenting Practices, and the Healthy Development of Children, *Depression in Parents, Parenting, and Children: Opportunities to Improve Identification, Treatment, and Prevention*, ed. Mary Jane England and Leslie J. Sim (Washington, DC: National Academies Press, 2009).

p. 26   *eating disorders have the highest mortality rate of any mental illness*: F. R. Smink, D. van Hoeken, and H. W. Hoek, "Epidemiology of Eating Disorders: Incidence, Prevalence, and Mortality Rates," *Current Psychiatry Reports* 14, no. 4 (2012): 406–14, https://www.ncbi.nlm.nih.gov/pubmed/22644309.

p. 27   *Among those suffering from anorexia, one in every five deaths is from suicide*: J. Arcelus et al., "Mortality Rates in Patients with Anorexia Nervosa and Other Eating Disorders: A Meta-analysis of 36 Studies," *Archives of General Psychiatry* 68, no. 7 (2011): 724–31, https://www.ncbi.nlm.nih.gov/pubmed/21727255.

p. 27   *thirty million people of all ages and genders suffer from an eating disorder*: Eating Disorders Coalition, Facts about Eating Disorders: What the Research Shows (2016), http://eating disorderscoalition.org.s208556.gridserver.com/couch/uploads /file/fact-sheet_2016.pdf.

p. 27   *Additionally, the National Association of Anorexia Nervosa publishes these statistics*: National Association of Anorexia Nervosa and Associated Disorders, "Eating Disorder Statistics," accessed January 24, 2019, https://anad.org/education-and-awareness /about-eating-disorders/eating-disorders-statistics.

p. 33   *peer victimization and bullying cause higher rates of suicide*: Mitch Van Geel, Paul Vedder, and Jenny Tanilon, "Relationship between Peer Victimization, Cyberbullying, and Suicide in Children and Adolescents," *JAMA Pediatrics* 168, no. 5 (2014): 435–42, https://jamanetwork.com/journals/jamapediatrics/fullarticle /1840250.

p. 33   *95 percent of teens own or have access to a smartphone*: Monica Anderson and Jingjing Jiang, "Teens, Social Media & Technology 2018," Pew Research Center, May 31, 2018, http://www .pewinternet.org/2018/05/31/teens-social-media-technology -2018.

p. 33   *the following statistics may not seem as shocking as they probably should*: StopBullying.gov, "Facts about Bullying," accessed November 15, 2018, https://www.stopbullying.gov/media/facts.

p. 43   *Cutting is the most common form of self-injury (and is used 70 to 90 percent)*: Mental Health America, "Self-Injury (Cutting, Self-Harm or Self-Mutilation)," accessed April 20, 2019, http://www.mentalhealthamerica.net/self-injury.

p. 44   *According to Teen Help, one-third to one-half of US adolescents*: "Cutting Statistics and Self-Injury Treatment," TeenHelp.com, accessed January 27, 2019, https://www.teenhelp.com/physical -health/cutting-statistics-and-self-injury-treatment.

p. 44   *on average as many as one in four girls aged fourteen to eighteen self-injure*: Martin A. Monto, Nick McRee, and Frank S. Deryck, "Nonsuicidal Self-Injury among a Representative Sample of US

Adolescents, 2015," *American Journal of Public Health* 108, no. 8 (August 1, 2018): 1042–48, https://www.ncbi.nlm.nih.gov /pubmed/29927642.

p. 49   *According to the National Center for PTSD, neglect is the leading cause*: This and other statistics in this section are from the US Department of Veterans Affairs, "PTSD: National Center for PTSD," accessed December 13, 2018, https://www.ptsd.va.gov /understand/common/common_children_teens.asp.

p. 51   *According to the American Psychological Association's Stress in America survey, today's teens*: American Psychological Associ- ation, *Stress in America: Generation Z* (October 2018), https:// www.apa.org/news/press/releases/stress/2018/stress-gen-z.pdf.

p. 55   *A 2015 Organisation for Economic Co-operation and Development study surveyed the well-being of teens*: "Most Teenagers Happy with Their Lives but Schoolwork Anxiety and Bullying an Issue," Organisation for Economic Co-operation and Development, April 19, 2017, http://www.oecd.org/newsroom/most-teenagers -happy-with-their-lives-but-schoolwork-anxiety-and-bullying -an-issue.htm.

p. 77   *The Partnership for Drug-Free Kids reports that 90 percent of addictions begin*: Pat Aussem, "What We Learned at Our Early- Intervention Parent Focus Groups," Partnership for Drug-Free Kids, March 13, 2019, https://drugfree.org/parent-blog/what-we -learned-at-our-early-intervention-parent-focus-groups.

p. 85   *according to a 2018 Pew Research report, 95 percent of US teens have access to a smartphone*: Anderson and Jiang, "Teens, Social Media & Technology."

p. 85   *According to one 2018 study, teens who spent more hours on a smartphone*: J.M. Twenge and W.K. Campbell, "Associations be- tween Screen Time and Lower Psychological Well-Being among Children and Adolescents: Evidence from a Population-Based Study," *Preventive Medicine Reports* 12 (October 2018): 271–83, doi:10.1016/j.pmedr.2018.10.003.

p. 95   *One study tracked 515 people who were saved before they jumped*: R.H. Seiden, "Where Are They Now? A Follow-up Study of Suicide Attempters from the Golden Gate Bridge," *Suicide &*

Life-Threatening Behavior 8, no. 4 (1978): 203–16, https://www
.ncbi.nlm.nih.gov/pubmed/217131.

p. 96   *Here is a list of suicide risk factors, according to the American
Foundation*: American Foundation for Suicide Prevention, "Risk
Factors and Warning Signs," accessed April 20, 2019, https://afsp
.org/about-suicide/risk-factors-and-warning-signs.

p. 100   *Girls attempt suicide twice as often as boys*: Suicide rates by
gender from "About Teen Suicide," Kids Health, last reviewed
August 2015, https://kidshealth.org/en/parents/suicide.html.

p. 101   *Teen suicide is on the rise. The number of suicides*: National
Education Association, "As Teen Suicide Rate Increases, States
Look to Schools to Address Crisis," NEAToday, May 14, 2018,
http://neatoday.org/2018/05/14/teen-suicide-prevention.

p. 101   *While girls between the ages of ten and fourteen make up a
small portion*: Sally C. Curtin, Margaret Warner, and Holly
Hedegaard, "Increase in Suicide in the United States, 1999–2014,"
National Center for Health Statistics, Centers for Disease
Control and Prevention, April 2016, https://www.cdc.gov/nchs
/products/databriefs/db241.htm.

p. 101   *In 2015, 18 percent of high school students seriously considered
suicide*: "Teen Suicide," Child Trends Databank, February 12,
2019, https://www.childtrends.org/?indicators=suicidal-teens.

p. 101   *About nine hundred thousand youths planned their suicides
during episodes*: Ginny Olson, *Teenage Girls: Exploring Issues
Adolescent Girls Face and Strategies to Help Them* (Grand Rap-
ids, MI: Zondervan/Youth Specialties, 2006).

p. 101   *Nearly 9 percent of high school students... Four out of five teens
who attempt suicide*: All the statistics between (and including)
these two quotes come from "Suicide Statistics," American
Foundation for Suicide Prevention, 2017, https://afsp.org
/about-suicide/suicide-statistics.

p. 102   *Ninety percent of teens who kill themselves have some type of
ongoing*: Jerry Reed, "90 Percent," Suicide Prevention Resource
Center, November 7, 2013, http://www.sprc.org/news/90-percent.

p. 102   *In any given year, one youth completes suicide for every twenty-
five*: "Teen Suicide," Stanford Children's Health, 2019, https://

www.stanfordchildrens.org/en/topic/default?id=teen-suicide
-90-P02584.

p. 103   *An NCAA survey found that 50 percent of college athletes started
steroid use*: "Substance Use: NCAA Study of Substance Use of
College Student-Athletes," National Collegiate Athletic Association, 2006, https://files.eric.ed.gov/fulltext/ED503214.pdf.

p. 122   *95 percent of the body's serotonin (the neurotransmitter responsible for regulating sleep)*: Siri Carpenter, "That Gut Feeling,"
Monitor on Psychology (American Psychological Association) 43,
no. 8 (September 2012), https://www.apa.org/monitor/2012/09
/gut-feeling.

WHERE TO GET HELP

When I say you are not alone, that is an understatement. There are literally hundreds of resources and organizations available with one goal in mind: your health and happiness. If you feel like you have nowhere to turn — or don't know how to help a friend — the following organizations offer resources for teens free of charge.

Teen Line: 310-855-4673, 800-852-8336, https://teenlineonline.org

If you have a problem or just want to talk with another teen who understands, Teen Line is a national hotline helping teenagers address their problems before they become a crisis. It's all about teens helping teens. This hotline is open every night from 6 PM to 10 PM PST. After hours, calls are directed to Didi Hirsh's Suicide Prevention Center.

Trevor Lifeline: 866-488-7386, www.thetrevorproject.org

The Trevor Project is specifically focused on helping LGBTQ youth and runs a 24/7 confidential hotline for anyone in crisis or experiencing suicidal thoughts.

National Eating Disorders Association: 800-931-2237, www.nationaleatingdisorders.org

This national helpline offers support for youth struggling with any type of eating disorder.

StopBullying.gov: www.stopbullying.gov

Learn how to stop bullying and get help by visiting Stop Bullying.gov.

Substance Abuse and Mental Health Services Administration (SAMHSA): 800-662-4357, www.samhsa.gov

SAMHSA runs a confidential, 24/7 hotline offering information and treatment options for individuals facing mental and/or substance abuse disorders.

Childhelp National Child Abuse Hotline: 800-422-4453, www.childhelp.org

Staffed 24/7, this hotline offers crisis intervention and support in over 170 languages for victims of child abuse or those who suspect child abuse is occurring.

National Suicide Prevention Lifeline: 800-273-8255, https://suicidepreventionlifeline.org

On this free, confidential, 24/7 hotline, your call will automatically be routed to a trained crisis worker who will listen and can tell you about mental health services in your area. Anyone struggling with mental or emotional issues — from self-harm to PTSD — should keep this number handy.

American Foundation for Suicide Prevention (AFSP): https://afsp.org

This amazing resource provides information, resources, and crisis intervention for anyone with suicidal thoughts or feelings, or those who fear for someone else.

National Alliance on Mental Illness (NAMI): 800-950-6264, www.nami.org

This hotline provides support, information, and referrals to anyone suffering from mental illness.

Crisis Text Line: Text 741741, www.crisistextline.org

When you're not up for talking, help is just a text away at this 24/7 counseling service.

DISCUSSION QUESTIONS

INTRODUCTION

1. How often do you, your friends, or your family members talk about suicide, depression, or mental illness?
2. What are some things in your life you feel you need to "keep up" with?
3. What would happen if you *didn't* keep up with these things?
4. Have you ever felt like you might have depression?
5. What are some ways social media makes you feel *bad*?
6. What are some ways social media makes you feel *good*?

CHAPTER 1: WHAT'S GOING ON IN YOUR BRAIN?

1. In what ways do teen brains differ from adult brains?
2. What are some reasons teens tend to be impulsive or reckless?

3. How do you think depression or mental illness can affect a teen's developing brain?
4. Why do you think teens are more susceptible to peer pressure and substance abuse than adults?

CHAPTER 2: YOU ARE NOT ALONE

1. Have you ever known someone going through a hard time and didn't know how to react?
2. What are some ways you can support someone who is struggling or in crisis?
3. What are some ways that others have supported you when you've been upset or struggled?

CHAPTER 3: DEPRESSION

1. What is something new in this chapter that you learned about depression?
2. Why do you think that most people who complete suicide suffer from depression?
3. Did this chapter's description of depression remind you of anyone (including yourself)? If so, in what ways?

Jackie's Story

1. What are some things Jackie experienced that could cause or worsen depression?
2. What are some things you related to, or didn't relate to, in Jackie's story?
3. What are some ways Jackie coped with her depression?
4. What could Jackie have done at a younger age to make her life better?

CHAPTER 4: EATING DISORDERS

1. What's the difference between diet and exercise and an eating disorder?
2. How do you think eating disorders serve as a coping mechanism for other issues?
3. Do you or someone you know have the risk factors or exhibit the symptoms of an eating disorder? How might you help them?

CHAPTER 5: BULLYING

1. What is the difference between bullying and other altercations or arguments?
2. Why do you think victims of bullying are more likely to think about suicide?
3. Have you ever been bullied? Have you ever bullied someone else?

Caitlin's Story

1. In your opinion, why didn't Sofia tell anyone about being bullied?
2. What are some of the warning signs of suicide Sofia exhibited?
3. If Sofia had been your friend, what would you have done to help?

CHAPTER 6: SELF-HARM

1. How is self-injury different than suicide or attempted suicide?

2. What are some reasons that people self-injure?
3. What are some of the warning signs or symptoms of self-injury?
4. Why is therapy and counseling so imperative for those who suffer from self-injury?

Kaley's Story

1. What social factors do you think influenced Kaley's self-injury?
2. Why do you think Kaley isolated herself from friends and family?
3. How did understanding self-injury empower Kaley to change?

CHAPTER 7: POST-TRAUMATIC STRESS DISORDER (PTSD)

1. Who suffers from PTSD?
2. How do you know if you have PTSD?
3. What are some of the risks of leaving PTSD untreated?
4. Who would you seek help from if you thought you had PTSD?

CHAPTER 8: PEER PRESSURE AND STRESS

1. What are some of the pressures you feel on a day-to-day basis?
2. Think about a time you gave in to peer pressure. What was your motivation?
3. How can the influence of peers be positive?

4. Why do you think some teens are more susceptible to peer pressure than others?
5. When have you ever found yourself doing something to please someone other than yourself?
6. What are some ways you can relieve stress?

CHAPTER 9: ANXIETY

1. Everyone gets anxiety now and then. What are some signs of an anxiety disorder?
2. Have you known anyone with an anxiety disorder? How did that affect his or her life?
3. Why are people with anxiety more likely to abuse drugs and alcohol?
4. What would you do if a friend or loved one showed signs of anxiety?
5. What are some ways you can curb anxiety?

Asher's Story

1. What or who were sources of pressure in Asher's life?
2. How did Asher's anxiety become a circular problem?
3. How did Asher's parents' situation add to his anxiety?
4. Did therapy cure Asher? How did it help him cope?

CHAPTER 10: SUBSTANCE ABUSE

1. What are some of the warning signs of drug and alcohol abuse?
2. Do you know anyone who has taken steroids?
3. Do you think they know the side effects?
4. Which, if any, of the steroid side effects surprised you?

5. Do you ever feel pressured to drink alcohol or take drugs?

6. Why do you think alcohol and drug abuse are linked to depression and suicide?

Connor's Story

1. By vaping e-cigarettes, how was Connor harming himself or increasing his risk of substance abuse?

2. Have you ever been offered drugs or alcohol? How did you react? What contributed to your decision?

3. Does your family have a history of alcoholism, drug abuse, or addiction?

4. Connor didn't want to do what others "told him" to do, but how did Connor's desire to make his own decisions backfire?

CHAPTER 11: TECHNOLOGY ADDICTION

1. How many hours each day do you use technology? Do you think you use it more or less than your peers?

2. Why do you think the risk of depression increases as screen time increases?

3. What are some ways you can self-regulate technology use?

4. When does social media make you feel happy, sad, and/ or anxious? Are there other feelings you associate with using social media?

5. How do you think your life and relationships would be different if you didn't have a smartphone or device?

Ethan's Story

1. Have you ever found video games, social media, or other technologies to be addictive?
2. Do you ever feel isolated, lonely, or depressed because of social media and technology use? Why?
3. How can a technology obsession be similar to a drug addiction?
4. Why did regulating technology use help Ethan's depression?

CHAPTER 12: SUICIDE

1. Has a friend, family member, or peer ever said anything about having suicidal thoughts? If so, what did you do?
2. Why do you think some people consider suicide?
3. After reading this book, what would you do if a friend told you they were considering suicide? Can you identify someone you might turn to for help?
4. Do you know anyone who currently displays any of the risk factors for suicide?

My Story

1. What were some warning signs of steroid use that Bill exhibited?
2. What risk factors of suicide did Bill have?
3. What effect might having friends who completed suicide have had on Bill?
4. What suicide warning signs did Bill exhibit?
5. In what ways might Bill's upbringing have impacted his substance-abuse problems and eventual suicide?

CHAPTER 13: FINDING HOPE IN THE DARKNESS

1. What does hope mean to you?
2. How can you strengthen your sense of hope?
3. Can you think of anyone in your life who needs hope?
4. After reading this book, how might you help them?

CHAPTER 14: CREATING A HEALTHY LIFESTYLE

1. What lifestyle changes could you make that would help you feel better mentally, emotionally, and physically?
2. Do you get regular exercise and practice good eating habits?
3. What are some things you do (or people you turn to) when you feel down?
4. How can you relax or unwind when you feel stressed out?

CHAPTER 15: REACHING OUT: HELPING A FRIEND

1. What are some of the ways your friends indicate, either verbally or nonverbally, that they are sad or depressed?
2. When has someone said something that made you feel better? What did they say, and why did it help?
3. When has someone said something hurtful? What did they say, and why was it painful?
4. If someone confessed to you that they were depressed, what are some positive things you might say, and what are some negative reactions to avoid?

INDEX

abuse, 48, 49, 96. *See also* child abuse; sexual abuse
academic performance: anxiety about, 62–65, 67; bullying and, 31, 35; depression and, 16, 21; hope and, 111; peer pressure and, 55; substance abuse and, 74, 78; suicide risk and, 98; technology addiction and, 83, 84
academic pressure, 6, 51, 55–56
acne, 79
addiction, 11, 75–77, 86–87, 134. *See also* alcohol/alcohol abuse; substance abuse; technology addiction
ADHD, 77
adults: brain of, teen brain vs., 7, 10, 129–30; getting help from, 36–37, 90, 100, 121, 136. *See also* parents

aggression, 48, 80, 97
agoraphobia, 68–69
alcohol/alcohol abuse: as anxiety risk factor, 67, 69; avoidance of, for healthy lifestyle, 126; as coping mechanism, 45, 76–77; as depression symptom, 21; developmental impact of, 71, 76–78; family history of, 69; GHB mixed with, 104; peer pressure and, 51; personal narratives, 72; as PTSD symptom, 49; as self-harm risk factor, 45; suicide risk and, 94, 102; teen statistics, 77; warning signs of, 78–79
alcoholism, 18–19, 77
alcohol paraphernalia, 79
American Foundation for Suicide Prevention (AFSP), 96–97, 147

ABOUT THE AUTHOR

Kristi Hugstad is on a mission to abolish the stigma of mental illness and suicide, and that starts with teens. Kristi's husband, Bill, completed suicide by running in front of a train after struggling for decades with clinical depression and substance abuse. Their story may have ended differently if they'd known the warning signs and risk factors of depression and suicide, and today Kristi is determined to raise awareness of both, so no one is ever too late to save a loved one.

Kristi Hugstad is the author of *What I Wish I'd Known: Finding Your Way through the Tunnel of Grief* and *R U OK?: Teen Suicide and Depression.* She is also a professional speaker, certified grief recovery specialist, grief and loss facilitator for addicts in recovery, and credentialed health educator. Kristi hosts *The Grief Girl* podcast and *The Grief Girl* OC Talk Radio show, and she is a longtime blogger for the *Huffington Post* and *Elephant Journal.* For more information, visit her website, www.thegriefgirl.com.